The South China
Sea Disputes

The South China Sea Disputes

Past, Present, and Future

Nalanda Roy

LEXINGTON BOOKS
Lanham • Boulder • New York • London

Published by Lexington Books
An imprint of The Rowman & Littlefield Publishing Group, Inc.
4501 Forbes Boulevard, Suite 200, Lanham, Maryland 20706
www.rowman.com

Unit A, Whitacre Mews, 26-34 Stannary Street, London SE11 4AB

British Library Cataloguing in Publication Information Available

Library of Congress Cataloging-in-Publication Data

Names: Roy, Nalanda, author.
Title: The South China Sea disputes : past, present, and future / Nalanda Roy.
Description: Lanham : Lexington Books, [2016] | Includes bibliographical references
    and index.
Identifiers: LCCN 2016038711 (print) | LCCN 2016038889 (ebook) | ISBN
    9781498536233 (cloth : alk. paper) | ISBN 9781498536240 (Electronic)
Subjects: LCSH: South China Sea—International status. | Territorial waters—Southeast
    Asia. | Maritime boundaries—Southeast Asia.
Classification: LCC KZA1692 .R69 2016 (print) | LCC KZA1692 (ebook) | DDC
    341.4/480916472—dc23

LC record available at https://lccn.loc.gov/2016038711

∞ ™ The paper used in this publication meets the minimum requirements of American
National Standard for Information Sciences—Permanence of Paper for Printed Library
Materials, ANSI/NISO Z39.48-1992.

Printed in the United States of America

Contents

Acronyms

A2/AD	Anti-access/Area denial
ACCF	ASEAN–China Cooperation Fund
ADMM	ASEAN Defense Ministers Meeting
ADMM Plus	ASEAN Defense Ministers Meeting Plus
ADR	Alternative Dispute Resolution
AEW&C	Airborne Early Warning and Control
AFP	Armed Forces of the Philippines
AMM	ASEAN Ministers Meeting
APEC	Asian Pacific Economic Cooperation
APT	ASEAN Plus Three
ARF	ASEAN Regional Forum
ASC	ASEAN Security Community
ASEAM-PMC	ASEAN Post-Ministerial Conference
ASEAN	Association of Southeast Asian Nations
ASEAN+1	ASEAN, China
ASEAN+3	ASEAN, China, Japan, South Korea
ASEAN-ISIS	ASEAN Institute of Strategic and International Studies
BP	British Petroleum
BTU	British Thermal Units
CAFTA	China–ASEAN Free Trade Agreement
CBM	Confidence Building Measure
CIDA	Canadian International Development Agency
CINCPAC	Commander-in- Chief of U.S. forces in the Pacific
CLCS	United Nations Commission on the Limits of the Continental Shelf
CMC	Central Military Commission
CNOOC	China's state-run China National Offshore Oil Company

CNP	China's comprehensive national power
CNPC	China National Petroleum Corporation
CS21	A Cooperative Strategy for 21st Century Sea Power
CSCAP	Council for Security cooperation in the Asia Pacific
CSI	Container Security Initiative
CSUA	Convention for the Suppression of Unlawful Acts
DFA	Department of Foreign Affairs
DOC 2002	Declaration on the Conduct of Parties in the SCS
DOD	U.S. Department of Defense
DRV	Democratic Republic of Vietnam
EEZ	Exclusive Economic Zone
EOR	Enhanced Oil Recovery
EU	European Union
FPDA	Five Power Defense Arrangements
FTA	Free Trade Area
GATS	General Agreement on Trade and Services
GEF	Global Environment Facility
GIS	Geographic Information System
GNP	Gross National Production
HPA	Hanoi plan of Action
HSC	High Seas Convention
ICAO	International Civil Aviation Organization
ICJ	International Court of Justice
IEA	International Energy Agency
IGO	Intergovernmental Organizations
IMB	International Maritime Bureau
IMO	International Maritime Organization
INCSEA	Incident at Sea
IOR	Indian Ocean Region
IPCC	Inter-governmental Panel on Climate Change
IR	International Relations
ISC	Information Sharing Center
ISDS	Institute of Strategic and Development Studies
ISM CT-TC	Inter-sessional Meeting on Counter-Terrorism and Transnational Crime
ISPS	International Ship and Port Security Code
ITLOS	International Tribunal for the Law of the Sea
JCG	Japanese Coast Guard
JDZ	Joint Development Zone
JMSU	Joint Maritime Seismic Undertaking
JMZs	Joint Management Zones
KM	Kilometers

LNG	Liquefied Natural Gas
LOSC	Law of the Sea Convention
MMCA	Military Maritime Consultative Agreement
MSC	Maritime Safety Committee
MSR	Marine Scientific Research
NAM	Non-aligned Movement
NIEs	Newly Industrialized Economies
NISCS	National Institute for the South China Sea Studies
NM	Nautical Miles
NOCs	National Oil Companies
NPCSD	North Pacific Co-operative Security Dialogue
NSR	Northern Sea Route
OECD	Organization for Economic Cooperation and Development
ONGC	Indian Oil and Natural Gas Corporation
OVL	ONGC Videsh
PDR	Lao People's Democratic Republic
PEMSEA	Partnerships in Environmental Management for the Seas of East Asia
PLA	People's Liberation Army
PLAN	People's Liberation Army Navy
PNOC	Philippine National Oil Company
POK	Pakistan occupied Kashmir
PPP	Public-Private Partnership
PSI	Proliferation Security Initiative
RECAAP	Regional Cooperation Agreement on Anti-Piracy in Asia
RIMPAC	Rim of the Pacific Exercise
RMSI	Regional Maritime Security Initiative
ROC	Republic of China (Taiwan)
SAP	Strategic Action Program
SAR	Search and Rescue
SCS	South China Sea
SDFs	Self-defense Forces
SEACAT	Southeast Asia Cooperation against Terrorism
SEANFWZ	Southeast Asia Nuclear Free Weapons Zone
SIGINT	Signals Intelligence
SKM	Square Kilometers
SLOCS	Sea Lines of Communication
SMA	Spratly Management Authority
SPR	Strategic Petroleum Reserve
SRV	Socialist Republic of Vietnam
TAC	Treaty of Amity and Cooperation in Southeast Asia
TCF	Trillion Cubic Feet

TPP	Trans-Pacific Partnership Free Trade Agreement
UN	United Nations
UNCLOS	United Nations Convention on the Law of the Sea
UNEP	United Nations Environment Program
UNESCO	United Nations Educational, Scientific and Cultural Organization
USEIA	US Energy Information Administration
VFA	Visiting Forces Agreement
WAB-21	Wan B8i-21 Block
WMD	Weapons of Mass Destruction
WTO	World Trade Organization
ZOPFAN	Zone of Peace, Freedom and Neutrality
ZOPFF/C	Zone of Peace, Freedom, Friendship and Cooperation

Chapter 1

Introduction

All warfare is based on deception. Hence, when able to attack, we must seem unable; when using our forces, we must seem inactive; when we are near, we must make the enemy believe we are far away; when far away, we must make him believe we are near. Hold out baits to entice the enemy. Feign disorder, and crush him.

—Sun Tzu, *The Art of War*

IMAGING SOUTHEAST ASIA

Situated between the southwest provinces of China and the east of India, Southeast Asia has long been of significant interest to scholars and its importance tends to grow not just politically and economically but also militarily. This region includes Brunei Darussalam, Cambodia, Indonesia, Lao People's Democratic Republic (PDR), Malaysia, Myanmar,[1] Philippines, Singapore, Thailand, Vietnam, and, arguably, the Democratic Republic of Timor-Leste. Besides being an important engine for global economic growth, Southeast Asia has also witnessed a plethora of important political changes and the emergence of new security threats. The end of the Cold War and the Cambodian conflict, closer relations between Vietnam and Association of Southeast Asian Nations (ASEAN) members, and the tentative rapprochement between Vietnam and China may have set the stage for a positive regional security relationship. However, historical mistrust, enduring territorial disputes, and competing maritime claims have combined to weaken an at least partially successful regional security structure.[2]

The Southeast Asian region and its surrounding water looks like a shatter-belt,[3] a strategically located region occupied by a number of competing states and caught between the conflicting interests of the extra-regional powers. The conflicting claims have changed the political fabric of this region. On the one hand, the South China Sea (SCS) acts as a sea bridge between the surrounding states, while on the other acts as an international thoroughfare in the world. In fact, the long-term prognosis is so demanding that in order to safeguard the vital sea-lanes and avoid possible conflicts, the Chinese dragon should reconcile to peaceful relationship in this region. Southeast Asian countries will face enormous challenges over the next decade. They will have to be competent not just in sustaining economic growth and addressing environmental issues, but they must also keep up with increasing energy demand and—and as this book emphasizes—manage potential conflicts in the SCS region.

Southeast Asia's position as a bridge between two oceans as well as between the continents of Asia and Oceania gives the region a distinctive identity and importance. It is not only an important area for trade and transport but it also includes vital sea lines of communication (SLOCs), which account for 32 percent of world oil net trade and 27 percent of world gas net trade.[4] This region has become a priority for China due to ongoing maritime disputes in the SCS along with her border conflicts with many countries of Southeast Asia. The current development challenges are an indication of dynamism, on the one hand, and vulnerability, on the other. Any carelessness may lead to severe negative developments and instability.[5] Moreover, we should remember "he bang xiang zheng, yu weng de li,' which means, "When the snipe and the clam grapple, it's the fisherman who profits."[6]

Before the twentieth century, the SCS was of little interest to any of the potential claimants. This region was not considered a particularly dangerous zone; however, this has obviously changed. During the 1930s, France came to the region and claimed both the Paracel and the Spratly Islands. Japan took charge following the defeat of France in World War II, and the SCS fell under the Japanese administrative system. After the withdrawal of Japan following the war, the importance of the SCS has been gradually recognized by its neighboring states. The SCS disputes mainly focus on two archipelagos: the Paracel and the Spratly Islands. All the claimant states in the SCS dispute have different bases for their claims to land features and maritime zones in this highly contested area. The claims to sovereignty over the various features in the SCS are mostly based on acts of discovery, historic use, and occupation. The emergence of the United Nations Convention on the Law of the Sea (UNCLOS) in the 1970s provided an incentive to put forward claims to huge maritime zones.[7]

PARTIES INVOLVED

China

Southeast Asia is the first region in which China has unleashed its soft power strategy.[8] In fact, this region also offers a window through which the world has witnessed China's growing influence. China's assertions of sovereignty in the SCS rest on historical claims of discovery and occupation. They date back to the twelfth-century Sung dynasty when references to the SCS were made in Chou Chu-fei's *Ling-Wai- tai-ta* or *Information on What Lies Beyond the Passes.* There are also references dating back to the eighteenth-century Qing dynasty.[9] Some records indicate that the Chinese marines discovered the Spratly Islands more than 2,100 years ago during the time of the Han Dynasty.[10] In fact China claims that it began to exercise jurisdiction over the Spratlys as early as the Ming Dynasty. Chinese records from the twelfth through the seventeenth centuries occasionally reference the islands and include maps.[11] From the nineteenth century onward, Chinese presence in the Spratly region has been documented when fishermen from Hainan and other parts of southern China often visited these islands. Records also indicate the presence of small-scale settlements in the Spratlys in the past.[12]

China, along with Taiwan and Vietnam, claim the Paracel Islands. All of the claims are based on a number of historical usages and prior discovery. Beginning in the nineteenth century to the early twentieth century, China made claims to the Paracel Islands without effective occupation.[13] Chinese ships sailed across the SCS 2,000 years ago and used the sea as a regular navigational route during the Han dynasty (206–220 A.D.). As Chinese voyages increased in frequency and range during the Tang Dynasty (618–906 A.D.), so did Chinese awareness of the Spratlys. Chinese archaeologists have even found some Chinese objects, which are considered to be evidence of China's ownership of the territories since ancient times.[14] An enormous amount of historical literature has also been presented by China to substantiate its claim.

In 1876, the first formal sovereignty claim was made when China's ambassador to England claimed the Paracel Islands as Chinese territory.[15] However, British troops destroyed several pirate camps located on some of the islands in the late eighteenth century[16] and, in 1877, the British claimed two territories in the area: the Spratly Islands and Amboyna Cay. Chinese authors assert that China has met the requirements found in the Isle of Palmas[17] arbitration by effectively exercising sovereignty over the Spratly islets without serious challenge for centuries until the French intruded in 1933. France first established a de facto physical control of seven of the larger territories and was followed by Japan in 1933.[18,19] By the end of March 1939, Japanese forces occupied and stationed troops on the Spratly Islands. They also put up a submarine base on both Itu Aba and Namyit Island in the Tizard Bank area.[20] Following the surrender of Japanese troops in 1945, Japan renounced all rights to the Spratlys in article 2 of the Treaty of Peace signed in 1951. Chinese naval patrols were then ordered to the Spratly Islands. China also protested and erased markers set by the French. Finally, in 1946–1947, China published official names for the islands and incorporated them into the Guangdong province.[21] The Peace Treaty, however, did not actually state who owned the Spratlys.

Although China claims the SCS islands "were always a part of Chinese territory,"[22] many commentators criticize this argument as weak. First of all, China's exercise of authority over the islands was only occasional and also Chinese records were unable to provide any compelling evidence of such effective occupation of the Spratlys.[23] The Chinese claim to the Spratly Islands was further weakened by a 1928 Chinese commission report, which stated that the Paracel Islands were the southernmost territory of China.[24] China appears to have had an interest in the Spratly Islands during different historical periods. However, no activity on the Chinese part could be characterized as "occupation" until 1988 when China built a marine observatory on Fiery Cross Reef.[25]

Taiwan

With the involvement of Taiwan in the SCS dispute, affairs became more complicated. Taiwan not only refers to itself as the Republic of China (ROC), but also historically insisted that it was the legitimate government of China.[26] The legal basis for Taiwan's claims in the SCS is China's long-standing historic ties to the islands. The ROC was the first government to establish a physical presence on the Spratlys when the Japanese withdrew following World War II. They have occupied the largest island in the Spratly group, Itu Aba, since 1956. Their unchallenged physical presence on this island for more than five decades may support a legal claim to sovereignty over the islands. However, other states have continuously rejected that claim.[27] The competing claims to the Spratlys were intensified after the outbreak of the Sino-Japanese war in the early 1930s. After this war, countries like Japan and France took advantage of Chinese weakness by occupying the Spratlys. Nevertheless, Taiwan maintained its sovereignty over the Spratlys in 1947 and even insisted that although the 1951 San Francisco Treaty did not include the Spratlys as part of Taiwan, its sovereignty over the Spratlys cannot be nullified.[28] In fact in 1993, Taiwan adopted a Policy Guideline for the SCS that asserted sovereignty over the Spratly Islands, the Paracel Islands, Macclesfield Bank, and the Pratas Islands. Besides, Taiwan claimed an exclusive economic zone (EEZ) of

200 nautical miles (nms) and the natural prolongation of the continental shelf in the Gulf of Tonkin.[29]

Brunei

Brunei currently claims two reefs, the first of which is Louisa Reef, also claimed by Malaysia, and Riflemen Bank. However, there is disagreement regarding Brunei's claims in the Spratlys. Some say that Brunei claims two territories in the Spratly group based on the prolongation of its continental shelf. Others argue that Brunei's only claim is to the continental shelf and an EEZ.[30] The Rifleman Bank claim was published by Brunei in a 1988 map, in which the extension of its continental shelf was based on a 350-nautical mile continental shelf claim. Brunei's claim to the Louisa Reef is weak because Louisa Reef only has two small rocks that are above water at high tide. Furthermore, these rocks do not have the capacity to generate an EEZ or continental shelf under article 121 (3) of UNCLOS.[31]

Vietnam

Vietnam asserts that it has maintained effective occupation of the two archipelagos (Paracel and Spratly Islands) at least since the seventeenth century when they were not under the sovereignty of any country and the Vietnamese state has exercised effectively, continuously, and peacefully its sovereignty over the two archipelagos until the time when they were invaded by the Chinese armed forces.[32] Vietnam argues that contact was first made with the Paracel Islands during the Nguyen dynasty (sixteenth to nineteenth centuries) and court documents from the reign of King Le Thanh Tong (fifteenth century) also prove that the Spratlys were at that time considered to be Vietnamese territory.[33] Heinzig states: "Vietnamese argumentation, covering the period until the end of the nineteenth century refers exclusively to the Paracels."[34] The Vietnamese government issued two white papers—one in 1979 and another in 1982—containing its compiled historical evidence regarding Vietnam's sovereignty over the Hoang Sa (or Paracel) and Truong Sa (or Spratly) archipelagos.[35] Vietnam's claim is based on rights of succession as the heir to the French colonial regime, which first occupied islands in the Spratlys in 1933.

France colonized Vietnam in the nineteenth century and hence occupied the Paracel Islands. However, the French claims were never accepted and thus the existence of any lawful title that allows Vietnam a claim by right of cession from France is unconvincing.[36] Vietnam has drawn straight baselines along its coast rather than laying down claims to maritime zones in the SCS. This arrangement raised objections from many states. Although the Chinese controlled the Paracel Islands after the Sino-Vietnam clash in 1974, Vietnam still maintains its territorial claims in this region. The strongest factor in Vietnam's favor is its physical possession and occupation of the largest number of Spratly islands and geographic formations.[37] However, Vietnam's evidence is also considered weak because it failed to specifically identify and distinguish between the Spratlys and the Paracels.

Philippines

The Philippines claim to most of the Spratly Islands is more recent than those of China and Vietnam and is based on a theory that the islands were *res nullius*, or abandoned, after World War II. The Philippines owned some of the islands either through discovery or prescriptive acquisition and maintains that its continental shelf extension also acts as a basis for its claim. The claim, however, does not meet the requirements of natural prolongation as stipulated in the UNLOS Convention.[38] Besides, the continental shelf provisions of the UNLOS Convention refers only to the seabed and subsoil, and it is not an instrument for claiming title to features that are permanently above the sea level.[39]

In 1947, a Filipino businessman and lawyer named Tomas Cloma "discovered" and established settlement in the islands. Cloma named them Kalayaan, or Freedomland, and appointed himself as the Chair of the Supreme Council. Cloma's declaration embraced an area extending from Palawan and included 53 territorial features.[40] The Philippine Foreign Secretary Carlos Garcia supported this declaration and in December 1956 issued the Garcia Declaration. According to this declaration, the area claimed by Cloma was to be regarded as *terra nullius*. This act triggered severe responses from South Vietnam, which immediately began occupying islands in the area.

China and France also challenged the claims; however, Cloma's occupation lasted only for a couple of months. Later, in 1971 and again in 1978, President Marcos formally declared the Kalayaan Island to be part of the Philippines.[41] Marcos also issued a separate Presidential Decree in 1978 claiming an EEZ around all the Philippine islands. This decree not only can be interpreted as including the Kalayaan islands but it also states that the Philippines' ratification of the Law of the Sea Convention "shall not in any manner impair or prejudice" its sovereignty over the Kalayaan Islands.[42]

Another branch of the *res nullius* claim is based on the 1951 San Francisco Peace treaty. According to the Philippines, under this treaty, the Spratlys were de facto under the trusteeship of the Allied Powers. They further argued that although Japan had acquired the islands, its sovereignty over the Spratlys was renounced in the 1951 San Francisco Treaty without ceding them to any other country. The Philippines has reinforced its *res nullius/occupation* claims by sanctioning drilling off the Reed Bank area since 1971 and by occupying eight of the territorial features since 1978. Their claims were criticized because Cloma's claim was neither approved nor disapproved by the Philippine government,[43] because Cloma's claim was neither approved nor disapproved by the Philippine government.[44] The 1955 government declaration on straight baselines around the Philippine archipelago did not include the Kalayaan area. Even the continental shelf claim is weak because the deep Palawan Trough that separates the Spratly Islands from the Philippine archipelago has no natural prolongation as required by article 76 of the UNLOS Convention.[45]

Malaysia

Malaysia is the only claimant that provides no historical records. Malaysia claims 12 islands and territorial features in the Spratly area and justifies its claim based on continental shelf extension and discovery/occupation. Malaysia's continental shelf claim arises out of the Geneva Conventions of 1958 pertaining to territorial waters and continental shelf boundaries.[46] Malaysia signed the convention in 1960 and passed its own Continental Shelf Act in 1966 and 1969, defining its continental shelf as "the seabed and subsoil of submarine areas adjacent to the coast of Malaysia up to 200 meters deep or the limit of exploitability."[47] In 1979, Malaysia published a "Map Showing the Territorial Waters and Continental Shelf Boundaries," thereby defining its continental shelf area and claiming all islands arising from it as its own.[48]

In 1983, Malaysia's Deputy Minister stated that Malaysia's claim to Amboyna Cay was simply a question of geography[49] and, in 1995, Malaysia's Prime Minister Mahathir visited Terembu Layang-Layang to reaffirm Malaysia's claim to this territory. Although Malaysia may have asserted this claim only in order to protect its other maritime zones, these claims are difficult to justify under continental shelf theory. Malaysian officials recognize their weaknesses in claiming sovereignty over islands based on the natural prolongation of the continental shelf and, hence, they tend to emphasize their claims based on discovery and occupation of the islands. However, Malaysia's claims are relatively recent and have been vigorously contested by other nations. In order to claim land as *res nullius*, a state must exercise effective control over it and not rely exclusively on discovery.[50]

Thus what we have found from the discussion so far is that the Chinese and Vietnamese claims loop around the Spratlys as well as the Paracels and overlap with the specific claims raised by the Philippines, Malaysia, and Brunei. The Philippine claim to Kalayaan overlaps with the Malaysian claim. Currently, Vietnam either occupies or has a presence on 27 territorial features. The Philippines claim nine territorial features. China also has a presence on nine featutes. Malaysia occupies three territorial features and has a presence on two other islands. Finally, Taiwan occupies only one island.[51]

ORGANIZATION

This book is best described as a policy-oriented analytical narrative targeting interested attentive-elite readers including academics and policy-makers. A qualitative historical-comparative methodology has been employed to help generate several qualitative research questions, to reinterpret data, and also to weigh established explanations. The book in its general approach parallels most of the existing literature, although of course—since the SCS situation has been rapidly evolving—this book is much more up-to-date in terms of information. From the knowledge generated by this study, other scholars may derive propositions, in addition to those formulated by the author—for further systematic empirical research and theoretical refinement.

The organization of this book is as follows. Chapter 1 provides a brief history of Southeast Asia, and its significance. This chapter also briefly describes the intended research area—the SCS—and surveys in a preliminary fashion the conflicts in the SCS. The chapter ends with an overview and purpose of different chapters.

Chapter 2 explains the strategic and economic importance of existing SCS disputes and assesses the effectiveness of UNCLOS as an international regime in addressing them. This chapter also focuses on the disputing parties, their reasons for engaging in specific disputes, and the current status of the disputes.

The next chapter reviews the history of the disputes during the Cold War and immediate post-Cold War period, including the involvement of other major powers in the region.

Chapter 4 discusses the involvement of China with other Asian claimants in SCS disputes, as well as "external" powers like the United States and India.

Chapter 5 weighs ASEAN's role in the development and functioning of Asia-Pacific multilateralism, and the extent to which ASEAN has been successful in creating a sense of regional community and addressing SCS disputes.

Finally, the last chapter summarizes the findings of the study, considers various policies that might at least help to lessen tensions in the SCS region, and suggests few lines of future research that might prove fruitful for policy-makers and/or academics.

NOTES

1. Burma was renamed Myanmar by the military government in 1989 and the name is recognized by the United Nations and most Asian countries.

2. Mark J. Valencia, Jon M. Van Dyke, and Noel A. Ludwig, *Sharing the Resources of the South China Sea* (Honolulu: University of Hawaii Press, 1999).

3. Chakraborti, P. 206; also refer Hawksley, Humphrey and Holberton, Simon. *Dragonstrike: The Millennium War* (Trans-Atlantic Publications, 1997).

4. Ibid., 56.

5. Niklas Swanstrom, ed. *Asia 2018–2028: Development Scenarios* (Sweden: Institute for Security and Development Policy, June 2008).

6. Guan, Ang Cheng, "ASEAN, China and the South China Sea Dispute," *Security Dialogue* 30, no. 4 (1999): 425.

7. The Law of the Sea, Official Text of the United Nations Convention on the Law of the Sea with Annexes and Index (UN Sales No. E.83.V.5, 1983).

8. Joshua Kurlantzick, *Charm Offensive—How China's Soft Power Is Transforming the World* (New Haven, CT: Yale University Press, 2007).

9. Christopher Joyner, "The Spratly Islands Dispute in the South China Sea: Problems, Policies, and Prospects for Diplomatic Accommodation," in *Investigating Confidence Building Measures in the Asia Pacific Region* Report 28. ed. Ranjeet Singh (Washington, DC: Henry L. Stimson Center, 1999).

10. Guoxing Ji, *The Spratly Disputes and Prospects for Settlement* (Kuala Lumpur, Malaysia: Institute of Strategic and International Studies,1992), 2–3.

11. Jon M. Van Dyke and Dal Bennett, "Islands and the Delimitation of Ocean Space in the South China Sea," *Ocean Yearbook* 10 (1993): 62.

12. R. Haller-Trost, "International Law and the History of the Claims to the Spratly Islands 10" (Paper presented at the South China Sea Conference, American Enterprise Institute, September 7–9, 1994), 11.

13. Shigeo Hiramatsu, "China's Advances in the South China Sea: Strategies and Objectives," *Asia-Pacific Review* 8, no. 1 (2001).

14. Lu Ning, *The Spratly Archipelago: The Origins of the Claims and Possible Solutions* (Washington, DC: International Center, 1993), 12.

15. Ibid., 64.

16. Wolfgang Schippke, "The History of the Spratly Islands in the South China Sea," http://www.southchinasea.org/docs/Schippke/1s0_h.html.

17. The Island of Palmas case involved a territorial dispute over the Island of Palmas between the Netherlands and the United States. It is one of the most highly influential precedents dealing with island territorial conflict.

18. Haller-Trost, "International Law and the History of the Claims to the Spratly Islands 10," 1994, 13.

19. Ibid., 15.

20. Ibid.

21. Daniel Dzurek, "The Spratly Islands Dispute: Who's On First?" *International Boundaries Research Unit Maritime Briefing* 2, no. 1 (1996).

22. Ji, *The Spratlys Disputes and Prospects for Settlements*.

23. Michael Bennett, "The People's Republic of China and the Use of International Law in the Spratly Island Dispute," *Stanford Journal of International Law* 28 (Spring 1992).

24. Dzurek, "The Spratly Islands Dispute: Who's On First?"

25. Valencia, Van Dyke, and Ludwig, *Sharing the Resources of the South China Sea*, 5.

26. Ibid., 29.

27. Joyner, "The Spratly Islands Dispute in the South China Sea," 1999.

28. Bob Catley and Makmur Keliat, *Spratlys: The Dispute in the SCS* (Singapore: Ashgate, 1997), 34.

29. Timo Kivimaki, ed. *War or Peace in The South China Sea?* 29.

30. Ji, *The Spratlys Disputes and Prospects for Settlements*, 9.

31. Valencia, Van Dyke, and Ludwig, *Sharing the Resources of the South China Sea*, 38.

32. Dzurek, "The Spratly Islands Dispute: Who's On First?" 11.

33. Valencia, Van Dyke, and Ludwig, *Sharing the Resources of the South China Sea*, 30.

34. Dzurek, "The Spratly Islands Dispute: Who's On First?" 8.

35. Joyner, "The Spratly Islands Dispute in the South China Sea," 201.

36. Ibid.

37. Valencia, Van Dyke, and Ludwig, *Sharing the Resources of the South China Sea*, 33.

38. Ibid., 35.

39. Joyner, "The Spratly Islands Dispute in the South China Sea," 203.

40. Leszek Buszynski, "Rising Tensions in the South China Sea: Prospects for a Resolution of the Issue," *Security Challenges* 6, no. 2 (Winter 2010).

41. Ibid.

42. Valencia, Van Dyke, and Ludwig, *Sharing the Resources of the South China Sea*, 33–35.

43. Van Dyke and Bennett, "Islands and the Delimitation of Ocean Space in the South China Sea."

44. Ibid.

45. Valencia, Van Dyke, and Ludwig, *Sharing the Resourcesof the South China Sea*, 35.

46. Convention on the Continental Shelf, April 29, 1958; Convention on the Territorial Sea and Contiguous Zone, April 29, 1958.

47. Haller-Trost, "International Law and the History of the Claims to the Spratly Islands 10," 32.

48. Valencia, Van Dyke, and Ludwig, *Sharing the Resources of the South China Sea*, 36.

49. Haller-Trost,"International Law and the History of the Claims to the Spratly Islands 10," 33.

50. Ibid., 6.

51. Buszynski, "Rising Tensions in the South China Sea."

Chapter 2

Reasons for Standoffs

Opportunities multiply as they are seized.

—Sun Tzu

PARTIES INVOLVED

As we have seen, the SCS has long been regarded as one of the most complex regional maritime systems in East Asia, and it has recently been the locus of disputes that have the potential of escalating into serious international conflicts. The SCS is a semi-enclosed sea bordered by member countries of the ASEAN, including Brunei, Cambodia, Indonesia, Singapore, Malaysia, Philippines, Thailand, and Vietnam. This area lies at the intersection of the world's most heavily traveled SLOCs—the east–west route connecting the Indian and Pacific Oceans and the north–south route connecting Australia and New Zealand to Northeast Asia.[1] This chapter surveys the significance of the SCS in terms of its strategic location, oil resources, and economic and marine biological diversity. It also reviews competing overlapping claims to the sea area by different countries, potential territorial disputes among the countries, and finally analyzes the relationships among these various issues.

There are four main island groups in the SCS: the Paracels, the Spratlys, the Pratas, and the Macclesfield Bank. Although the Natunas, a fifth group of islands, is not considered part of the SCS, they are worth mentioning because Indonesia and Vietnam are in dispute over the continental shelf of these islands. Before the end of the Cold War, the presence of both the Russian as well as the United States navy facilities in Vietnam and the Philippines largely provided a stabilizing balance of power in the region.

However, their withdrawal from this region has made China the dominant naval force. Neighbors fear that Beijing is trying to establish the entire region as a "Chinese Lake."[2] According to Rosenberg, three movements—resource control, the conservation movement of environmentally sustainable resources, and the security movement—contribute to the growing importance of the SCS region. Territorial claims to the islands and reefs are especially important in order to establish an EEZ around the disputed islands that would include the oil and natural gas resources in the area. The SCS has numerous archipelagos, islands, peninsulas, coral reefs, seasonally reversing monsoon winds, and underwater currents. All these combine to produce exceptionally favorable conditions for a fertile marine ecosystem.[3]

The Spratly Islands are known in Vietnam as the Truong Sa and in China as the Nansha. The Paracel islands are known as the Hoang Sa in Vietnam and the Zhongsha in China, the Pratas are known as the Dongsha in China, and the Macclesfield Bank is known as the Quandao Trung Sa in Vietnam or Zhongsha Qundao in China. Current and potential disputes involve maritime powers like China; archipelago states like Indonesia and the Philippines; strait states like Malaysia and Indonesia; Thailand, which is not part to the UNCLOS; and strait user states such as the United States and Japan, among others. This chapter will later discuss how the composition of this dispute reflects several dimensions of the UNCLOS. Table 2.1 shows claims by countries in the region.

THE NINE-DOTTED LINE CONTROVERSY

One of the most difficult issues impacting upon sovereignty claims and disputes in the SCS is the "dotted" or "the nine-dotted line" found on Chinese

Table 2.1   Claims by Countries in the Region

Country	South China Sea	Spratly Islands	Paracel Islands	Gulf of Thailand
Brunei	UNCLOS	no formal claim	no	n/a
Cambodia	not applicable (n/a)	n/a	n/a	UNCLOS
China	all*	all	all	n/a
Indonesia	UNCLOS	no	no	n/a
Malaysia	UNCLOS	3 islands	no	UNCLOS
Philippines	Significant portions	8 islands	no	n/a
Taiwan	all*	all	all	n/a
Thailand	n/a	n/a	n/a	UNCLOS
Vietnam	all*	all	all	UNCLOS

*Excluding buffer zone along littoral states (calculations for buffer unknown)
(Adapted from U.S. Energy Information Administration, South China Sea [Analysis Brief], http://www.eia. gov/countries/regions-topics.cfm?fips=SCS, March 2008.)

maps dating back to 1947. That year, the Nationalist government of Chiang Kai-shek defined China's claims by an area limited by nine dots covering most of the SCS. And, in 1951, Zhou Enlai formalized this claim.[4] This line is also known as the "U-shaped line." Opinions vary regarding the legality of this "U-shaped" line in the SCS. In the year 1935, "The Map of Chinese Islands in the South China Sea," published by the Land and Water Maps Inspection Committee showed that China's southernmost boundary reached latitude 4° north and that the James Shoal was marked within the Chinese boundary.[5] Although there is no exact definition in international law for the concept of historic title, its legitimate basis for claiming sovereignty is well recognized. For example, article 15 of the 1982 UNCLOS stipulates that the delineation rule for overlapping territorial sea claims "does not apply . . . where it is necessary by reason of historic title or other special circumstances to delimit the territorial seas of the two States in a way which is at variance with this provision."[6]

In an article titled "International Recognition of China's Sovereignty over the Nansha Islands," published in the year 2000, the Chinese Foreign Ministry claimed that various nations acknowledged and recognized the Nansha Islands as Chinese territory. Lee Lai To stated that China's historical records, maps, and cultural relics support the country's historical claims to these islands.[7] However, the British scholar Andrew Forbes argued that he did not find a place where the Chinese explorers mentioned the Spratlys. Rather, he found only the name of the Paracel Islands.[8] In fact no one paid much attention to the Spratlys until World War II when the Japanese started using this island for military purposes. Taiwan has reportedly deemed "the entire area within the U-shaped line to be China's historical waters."[9] According to Zou Keyuan, historic rights fall into two types: exclusive with complete sovereignty, such as historic waters and bays, and nonexclusive without complete sovereignty, such as historic fishing rights in the high seas.[10] However, Keyuan argues that historic rights claimed by China are unique and different from these types because they are connected with the EEZ/continental shelf regimes.[11] He calls the situation "historic rights with tempered sovereignty," whereby China can claim sovereign rights and jurisdiction, but not complete sovereignty.[12] Some scholars, like Keyuan, contend that since the declaration of the nine-dotted line, international society made no diplomatic protests nor voiced any disagreements.[13] Later, a number of maps produced abroad were delineated along the nine-dotted line indicating the area as belonging to China. China claims ownership and historic right to islands, reefs, shoals, banks, and waters within the nine-dotted line. In 1979, Hasjim Djalal wrote,

> The nature of the claim of the PRC to the South China Sea is enigmatic . . . It is not clear whether the lines indicated in the Chinese maps are intended as the

limits of the Chinese territorial claim towards the whole area, thus including the islands, the sea, the airspace, the seabed and all the resources contained therein; or whether the lines simply indicate that only the islands contained within the lines which are claimed by the PRC. Careful reading of the Chinese statements on this matter, especially those at the ICAO meetings (1979), indicates that the Chinese territorial claims are limited to the islands and all rights related thereto, and not territorial claims over the South China Sea as a whole.[14]

The Chinese government has attempted to substantiate this claim with the help of many other "official maps, e.g. Huang Qing GeZhi Sheng Fen Tu (Map of the Provinces Directly Under the Imperial Authority), which was made in the twentieth year of Qianlong (1755); Da Qing Wan Nian YiTong Di Li QuanTu (map of the Eternally Unified Great Qing empire) made in the fifteenth year of Jiaqing (1810); and Da Qing Yi Tong Xia QuanTu (map of the Unified Territory of the Great Qing empire) made in the twenty-second year of the Jiaqing (1817)."[15] Historically, China considered the SCS as part of its Southern China sea and hence it was named Nan Hai, which means South Sea. China's strategic thinking about this region is largely influenced by Deng Xiao-ping's "Eight Principles of International Strategic Thinking," which was largely used by Jiang Zemin's third generation leadership as the basis for China's foreign policy.[16]

In fact the recent publication of the book, "The Nine-Dash Line in the South China Sea: History, Status, and Implications," by the China Institute for Marine Affairs has generated further concerns among its neighbors. The book explores a historical line of maritime rights over the disputed waters, and also puts forth arguments on China's so-called right to fishing and the right to explore in waters covered by the dotted line. Besides, the publication of China's new national map that incorporates a 10th "dash" located to the east of Taiwan has created ripples in Southeast Asia and beyond. In fact Beijing's recent inclusion of the area around Natuna in its newly sanctioned maps (and on Chinese passports) has also generated tension in the region. Overtime it has become really difficult to connect Beijing's speculative dashes.

HISTORICAL CLAIMS AND COUNTERCLAIMS

The Paracels

The Paracels, whose ownership is contested by China, Taiwan, and Vietnam, consist of fifteen islands, several sand banks, and reefs. The area lies between latitude 16° and 17° north and longitude 111° and 113° east. The group is located less than 150 nms from China's Hainan islands and about 240 nm from Daning in Vietnam. This archipelago has an area of about 15,000 square kilometers (skm) and is divided into two clusters: the eastern cluster of An Vinh and the western cluster of Luoi Liem. There are two main groups: the Amphitrites and the Crescent, which lie some 70 kilometers (km) from one another. In the west, the Crescent Group consists of five main islands: Robert Island, Duncan Island, Palm Island, Drummond Island, and Pattle Island.[17] Money Island lies 12 km away and Triton Island is further south. To the west lies the Amphitrite group, which consists of Woody Island, Rocky Island, South Island, Middle Island, North Island, and Tree Island. To the east of this group lies the Lincoln Islands. Woody Island, the largest in the group, is 4 km long and 2 to 3 km wide. The distance from east to west and from north to south of the archipelago is about 95 and 90 nm respectively.[18] Having ousted the South Vietnamese in 1974, China now occupies all of the Paracels and today has an airfield on Woody Island in the Paracels.

The Pratas and Macclesfield Bank

Taiwan has occupied Itu Aba Island since 1956 and had plans to build a 6,500-foot runway, an air terminal, a lighthouse, and fishing port on the island in order to exercise its control.[19] Pratas Island is 6 km in length and 2 km in width. Because it is shaped like the moon, it is also known as Moon Island. There are two small banks—south vereker and north vereker. The island is located between latitude 20°30' and 21°31' north and longitude 116° and 117° east.[20] The Macclesfield Bank is located at latitude 15°20' north and longitude 113°40' to 115°east. The bank is about 75 nm long and 33 nm wide.[21]

The Spratlys

According to Prescott, "There is no single authoritative definition of the extent of the Spratly Islands, but they are found in the southeastern part of the South China Sea."[22] Heinzig defined it as the area lying between latitude 4° and 11°30' north and longitude from 109°30' to 117°50' east.[23] China's Xinhua News Agency published a partial definition in the year 1991, according to which,

> The Nansha Archipelago [Spratly Islands] (in ancient times called WanliShi-tang) is located from 3 degree 37' to 11 degree 55' north latitude to 109 degree 43' to 117 degree to 47' east longitude, stretching south to north approximately 550 (nm), and spreading east to west more than 650 (nm); its water territory area exceeds 800,000 square kilometers.[24]

The Spratlys are of strategic, maritime and economic importance because they lie amidst the principle SLOCs for commercial ships transiting the

Indian and Pacific Oceans (that is, the straits of Malacca, the Singapore Strait, the Sunda Strait, and the Lombok Strait). They were named after Richard Spratly, the captain of a British whaler, *Cyrus South Seaman*, who reportedly explored the islands in 1843.[25] The Spratly archipelago is a group of more than 230 islets, reefs, shoals, and sand banks scattered over an area of about 160–180,000 skm. The main island, North Danger Group, is composed of four islets including Trident Shoal, Lys Shoal, ThiTu, and Subi Reef. Tizard Bank is of two main islands and three reefs, including the Itu Aba Island.[26]

The coast point of Spratly archipelago is about 250 nm from the Hainan island of China. The distance from east to west and from north to south is about 325 and 274 nm respectively.[27] This region was sometimes referred to as the "Dangerous Ground" to warn sailors about uncharted coral reefs because it lacked any formal name. The government of the Philippines generally calls the Spratly islands "Kalayaan" or "Freedomland." This Philippine portion includes islands that lie west of Palawan and north of latitude 7°40' north. Its northern limit is latitude 12° north and its eastern limit is longitude 111° east. Although the Spratly Islands have neither indigenous inhabitants nor any type of established economic activity, still they have become the fulcrum for energy competition and conflicting claims in the Asia-Pacific region.[28] It is also one of the richest fishing grounds in the world.

This area has become critical among the disputing countries mainly because of its geographic position in major oceanic routes used by crude oil tankers from the Persian Gulf to Asia, routes for goods from Asia to the rest of the world, and promising offshore oil and gas reserves. The Spratly seabed is thought to contain the greatest concentration of oil and gas reserves within the SCS.[29]

Ninety percent of Japan's oil passes through this area[30] and China has called the sea a "second Persian Gulf."[31] Estimates of the oil resources near the Spratly Islands range from 105 billion barrels to 213 billion barrels.[32] Estimates of total gas reserves also vary from 266 trillion cubic feet (TCF) to more than 2,000 (TCF). Regarding the Spratly issue, Beijing continues to move forward with a "three no's" policy—no specification of claims, no multilateral negotiations, and no internationalization of the subject.[33] China has even consolidated its facilities at Fiery Cross Reef in the Spratly archipelago with the installation of an early warning radar system. At the same time, China maintains a continuing naval presence at Mischief Reef off the west coast of the Philippines.[34]

As Asia's energy consumption grows in parallel with its economic development, access to and control of these resources will weigh heavily on claimant perceptions of the strategic value of contested areas[35]—not least the Spratlys. The wider significance of disputes in the SCS relates to the threat that a higher level of military action could pose to vital SLOC arteries to other parts of the world, including the Middle East. If the SLOC get disrupted due to armed conflict, then the economic interests of the Asia-Pacific countries as well as the United States could be severely affected.[36] Over half of the top ten container shipping ports in the world are located in or around the SCS, which is the main artery of transportation for imports and exports. In fact, it is not too much to say that this region has become the hub of the industrial revolution of Asia.[37] Besides safety of navigation, overflight is of critical strategic interests to the United States. This is because the United States uses the SCS both as a transit point and an operating area for its Navy and Air Force facility between military bases in Asia and the Indian Ocean and Persian Gulf areas.[38] In other words, the multicountry character of the Spratly Islands dispute has made it perhaps the most complicated of territorial disagreements.[39]

China's claiming of the Spratly Islands comes from its early discovery of the islands during the Qing dynasty (1644–1911). However, Livingstone argues that according to international law, mere discovery is not enough to claim sovereignty over a territory.[40] However, in 1992, China passed a sea and zone act to enforce its legal claim to the Spratlys. Article 2 of the legislation specifically identified the Spratlys as Chinese territory.[41] The Chinese have had garrisons on seven Spratly islets since 1988. Although China's stated aim is to promote a harmonious world of enduring peace and common prosperity,[42] factors such as rapid economic growth and rising energy demand have made it important for them to ensure the safety of vital SLOC. In fact, their naval modernization is viewed by some as an effort to overcome the "Malacca dilemma"—the threat to China's national security posed by the potential closure of narrow straits or choke points in Southeast Asia.[43]

The Vietnamese claim the Spratly Islands because of their historical ties to the Nguyen (1803–1945) dynasty. Their claim is also based in part on their colonial relationship with France and the French claim to the Spratlys in 1933. The Spratlys were returned to the French at the end of the World War II. By 2000, Vietnam had stationed 600 troops on at least 27 Spratly land formations.[44] The Philippines justify their claim over the Spratlys because of the discovery of certain islands by the Filipino citizen Thomas Cloma in 1947. Cloma asserted ownership of 33 islands, reefs, and fishing grounds within an area covering 65,000 sq. nm. He even coined the term "Kalayaan," or "Freedomland," for the area and sent a letter to the Philippine vice president requesting official endorsement. The Philippine government observed that the Kalayaan Islands were *res nullius* and open to exploitation by Filipinos since no country had established sovereignty.[45] The islands were annexed in 1978 by the Philippine government and were thereafter administered by them because they lie within their EEZ.[46] Currently, they have marines stationed on eight islands and some 50 islets, reefs, and shoals.[47]

Situated 240 km west of Palawan Island in the main Philippines archipelago is the horseshoe-shaped Mischief Reef, which is 9 km in length and 6 km in width. It is claimed by China, Taiwan, and Vietnam. Because it gets submerged during high tides, it does not qualify as an island under the 1982 UNCLOS for purposes of maritime jurisdiction. It is often debated that an Alcorn petroleum agreement between Manila and its American subsidiary in 1994, as well as military cooperation between Manila and Hanoi, may have instigated China's occupation of the Mischief Reef. Exchange visits at the highest level between Hanoi and Manila were regarded by Beijing as threatening.[48] Although the Philippines tried to gain support from the United States under the U.S.–Philippine Mutual Defense Treaty, they were rebuffed by the United States because the reef lies in the Kalayaan area. Tensions rose after China occupied Mischief Reef in 1995. This incident led to the 2002 ASEAN–China Declaration on the Conduct of Parties in the SCS. See Appendix 1 the 2002 ASEAN–China Declaration on the Conduct of Parties.

Malaysia and Brunei have asserted claims to certain islands and reefs based on articles 76 and 77 that define the limits of a coastal state's continental shelf under the UNCLOS.[49] Malaysia is the most recent claimant to occupy part of the Spratlys militarily. Brunei is the only claimant without a military presence in the Spratlys.[50] However, Brunei currently claims two reefs: Louisa Reef (which is also claimed by Malaysia) and Riflemen Bank, which is apparently based on a 350 nm continental shelf claim.

Brunei also claimed a 200 nm fishing zone and a 200 nm EEZ in 1984. However, Brunei's claim for the Louisa Reef is weak, since the Reef has only two small rocks that alone are incapable of generating an EEZ or continental shelf under article 121(3) of UNCLOS.[51] Taiwan's claim suffers from the same issues as that of China because its legal basis for sovereignty rests on historic ties to the islands. Taiwan, in fact, adopted a policy guideline for the SCS on March 1993 that asserted sovereignty over the Spratly Islands, the Paracel Islands, Macclesfield Bank, and the Pratas Islands. Taiwan also argued, "The SCS area within the historic water limit is the maritime area under the jurisdiction of the Republic of China, in which the Republic of China possesses all rights and interests."[52] Thus, Taiwan was the first government to establish a physical presence on Spratly and has occupied the largest island named Itu Aba since 1956.[53]

UNITED NATIONS CONFERENCE ON
THE LAW OF THE SEA (UNCLOS)

Although the SCS is much greater in area than the Arabian Gulf or Caspian Sea, it is similar to both these regions in two respects. First, its undersea resources are subject to overlapping claims and, second, the countries became involved in maritime disputes to protect their perceived national interests.[54] The SCS dispute embodies two dimensions: territorial sovereignty and jurisdictional rights under maritime demarcation arising from differing interpretations following the 1982 UNCLOS.[55] The First United Nations Conference on the Law of the Sea (UNCLOS I) adopted four conventions commonly known as the 1958 Geneva Conventions: (a) The Convention on the Territorial Sea and Contiguous Zone; (b) The Convention on the High Seas; (c) The Convention on Fishing and Conservation of the Living Resources; and (d) The Convention on the Continental Shelf. Although considered to be a step forward, the conventions did not establish a maximum breadth of the territorial sea.[56] In 1960, the Second United Nations Conference on the Law of the Sea (UNCLOS II) was held, which did not result in any new international agreements. Once again, it neither failed to fix a uniform breadth for the territorial sea nor did it establish consensus on sovereign fishing rights. Finally, the Third United Nations Conference on the Law of the Sea (UNCLOS III) was held from 1973 to 1982.[57] It addressed earlier issues and came into force on November 14, 1994, creating what is sometimes regarded as the constitution for the oceans.

Maritime boundary disputes are those relating to the delimitations of the sea areas over which the coastal states can exercise jurisdiction in conformity with both international law and the law of the sea. Traditionally, the maritime zones are grouped into three categories: internal waters, territorial sea, and the contiguous zone. The sovereignty of a coastal state extends, beyond its land territory and internal waters to an adjacent belt of sea, described as territorial sea. Sovereignty extends to airspace over the territorial sea and to its seabed and subsoil. The maximum breadth of the territorial sea is 12 nms (a nautical mile is 6,076 feet long), and is measured from a nation's baselines.[58] This reflected the struggle between two conflicting trends of thought in the law of the sea that emerged in seventeenth century. They are freedom of the sea, as represented by Hugo Grotius, and the dominion of the sea, supported by John Selden, a British author who argued for the right of states to extend their jurisdiction over the sea.[59]

According to the customary international law that gradually evolved, the territorial sea was three miles from shore. The first international attempt to codify the breadth of the territorial sea was at the 1930 Hague Conference held under the auspices of the League of Nations. The continental shelf doctrine, holding that a country has exclusive control over waters above its continental shelf, was proclaimed by the U.S. President Truman in 1945 and was subsequently adopted at the First United Nations Conference on the Law of the Sea. However, the concept of an EEZ of 200 miles from the shoreline or other line drawn according to treaty specifications was introduced for the

first time in 1971 by Kenya at the Asian–Africa Legal Consultative Committee held in Nigeria and was finally accepted at the Third UNCLOS in 1982.[60]
The EEZ is a maritime area beyond and adjacent to the territorial sea in which
the coastal state has sovereign rights and jurisdiction. These rights are less
than full sovereignty, and all states have freedoms of navigation and overflight in EEZ. The maximum breadth of the EEZ is 200 nms from baselines
from which the breadth of the territorial sea is measured.[61] Appendix 2 gives
a description of the EEZ rules under Part V of the UNCLOS.[62]

The potential riches of the SCS and its adjacent waters have increased
competition and conflicts, and thus it might be said that the Asian theater
will be critical for shaping state practice regarding the law of the sea and
determining whether or not the 1982 convention will really constitute the
law in being.[63] The 1982 convention has been ratified in the region only by
Indonesia, Philippines, and Vietnam. Nonetheless, the UNCLOS rules, especially those relating to the EEZ, have converted the entire region into the most
extensively claimed area in the world.[64] Considered as a complex ocean gov-
ernance system, the UNCLOS has 17 parts, 320 articles, and nine annexes.
The question has arisen whether article 121 (paragraph 2) of the UNCLOS is
applicable to these islands, islets, and rocks, that is, whether the annexation
of the archipelagos in itself gives exclusive rights to the living resources of
the sea within the limit of 200 nm. In addition, the situation is more complex
because coastal states can also be straits states, archipelagic states, or even
geographically disadvantaged states.[65] For example, Singapore is both a
maritime user as well as a straits state. Article 121 (paragraph 2) also states,
"Except as provided for in paragraph 3, the territorial sea, the contiguous
zone, the exclusive economic zone and the continental shelf of an island are
determined in accordance with the provisions of this Convention applicable
to other land territory."[66] Yet, paragraph 3 of the same article states, "Rocks
which cannot sustain human habitation or economic life of their own shall
have no exclusive economic zone or continental shelf."[67] Here is the crux of
some current disputes. Such features are only entitled to a 12-nm territorial
sea and a 500-meter safety zone, respectively. Since the UNCLOS terms
seem to apply to most features in the Spratly archipelago, it is often debated
as to whether most of the Spratly Islands are sufficient to establish a legitimate basis for maritime jurisdiction.[68]

Disputes associated with the SCS actually involve almost every aspect
mentioned in the UNCLOS, for example, maritime delimitation, historic title,
territorial sovereignty, use of force, military activities, fishing, marine scientific research (MSR) and environment protection, freedom of navigation, and
even deep seabed mining.[69] Thus it might be said that the very convention that
was designed to allow countries defined access to ocean spaces encouraged
states to make more claims and thus generated even more disputes.

REASONS BEHIND THE CONFLICT

The SCS dispute has an obvious geostrategic dimension. If China ever suc-
ceeds in realizing its territorial claims, it would then "extend its jurisdiction
some one thousand nautical miles from its mainland so as to command the
virtual Mediterranean or maritime heart of Southeast Asia with far-reaching
consequences for the strategic environment."[70] Each state has developed
apparently irreconcilable positions regarding islands and archipelagos.
According to Garver, Lebensraum ideas have strongly influenced Chinese
policy in the SCS since the late 1970s.[71] The Japanese demonstrated the
strategic importance of this area during World War II when they used the
Spratlys as a submarine base. The SCS has acquired added significance since
it harbors large energy reserves. Thus it has become quite impossible for the
claimants to follow the "good fences make good neighbors" policy at least in
the sea.[72] Furthermore, most of the East Asian countries use a straight baseline system[73] to calculate boundaries and are criticized for distortion due to
the liberal interpretation of UNCLOS article 7.[74]

One basis for China's claim to the waters of the SCS, as previously mentioned, is its supposed historic title. Although the UNCLOS Convention does
not define the legal regime of historic title or historic waters, it recognizes
these regimes in articles 10(6), 15, and 46(b). Construction of China's Yulin
Naval Base near Sanya on Hainan Island enhanced its strategic significance
for the balance of power in the region. This base will provide China with
the capability to extend the People's Liberation Army Navy (PLAN's)
military reach into the Pacific Ocean and SCS. The docks at Yulin Naval
Base currently hold several major surface warships and nuclear submarines.
The apparent Chinese intention is to enhance its capability to exercise its
sovereignty claims over the SCS and protect its vital SLOCs. This base will
considerably shorten the logistics tail for PLAN forces that are deployed into
the SCS. At the same time, China will have the capacity to threaten the same
SLOCs on which Japan, Taiwan, and South Korea are dependent.

Much of the base is built underground so that facilities cannot be eas-
ily monitored by satellite. It is capable of housing nuclear submarines like
the Type-094 submarine, a second-generation nuclear vessel representing
China's most lethal naval strike weapon.[75] Previously all nuclear submarines
were under the command of China's North Sea Fleet. However, this base
marks the first permanent deployment to China's South Sea Fleet. It provides
China with the capability to station a substantial proportion of its submarine-
based nuclear deterrent force here. Chinese nuclear subs operating from
Yulin will be able to patrol and fire from concealed positions in deep waters
off Hainan Island if China can develop the necessary operational skills. This
might threaten the general naval balance of power in the SCS. China has also

developed anti-access/area denial (A2/AD) capabilities to challenge the U.S. Navy in this region.[76] Since China is a key regional player, any movement by the Chinese invariably generates tension. For example, in January 2010, U.S. Admiral Robert Willard said, "[T] he Chinese navy had increased its patrols in the South China Sea and had shown an increased willingness to confront regional nations on the high seas and within the contested island chains."[77]

There are three kinds of maritime disputes in East Asia: territorial disputes over tiny islets, maritime boundary delimitation disputes between neighboring states, and disputes over the allocation and sustainable use of marine resources. It is difficult to have a plausible solution for the first kind of dispute since the disputing states have asserted sovereignty claims over the islands. The maritime boundary delimitation set out in the UNCLOS is also a source of tension between China and its neighbors. Although China and Vietnam have signed the agreement on the maritime boundary delimitation in the Gulf of Tonkin, there is no other maritime boundary agreement between China and other neighboring countries.[78] The only noticeable progress is in the management of marine natural resources in the East China Sea, the Yellow Sea, and the Sea of Japan. The SCS is rich in both living and nonliving resources. Fishing remains an important economic activity in this region. The SCS provides 25 percent of the protein needs for 500 million people and 80 percent of the Philippine diet.[79] Several agreements were signed between neighboring states for the proper management of this industry. For example, the Fishery Agreement between China and Japan signed in 1997, the Japan-South Korea Fishery Agreement in 1998, and the 2000 China–South Korea Fishery Agreement.[80]

As far as the nonliving resources are concerned, as has been stressed, this region is widely known for its rich oil and gas reservoirs. In March 2002, the German Chamber of Commerce published a report stating that the SCS is also rich in tin, manganese, copper, cobalt, and nickel. The report further estimated that there are 70,000 tons of phosphorous in the Spratly regions.[81] The discovery of oil and gas reservoirs in the West Pacific has made Indonesia one of the world's leading oil exporting states. Both onshore and offshore petroleum has given Brunei the highest per capita gross national product (GNP) in the region. The 1995 assessment made by Russia's Research Institute of Geology of Foreign Countries declared that the Spratly Islands might contain 6 billion barrels of oil equivalent, of which 70 percent would be natural gas.[82] Southeast Asia's first offshore well was drilled in 1957. However, the race for oil actually started in 1969–1970 when an international report by the Committee for the Coordination of Joint Prospecting for Mineral Resources in Asian Offshore Areas declared the prospect of finding huge reserves of oil and gas in the SCS.[83] Brunei, Malaysia, and Vietnam were already oil producers. In 1993, China became a net energy importer.

Malaysia is operating in the Central Luconia gas fields off the coast of Sarawak. The Philippines are operating northwest of Palawan in the Camago and Malampaya fields. Indonesia has the Natuna gas field. British Petroleum (BP) is operating the LanTay and Lan Do gas fields in Vietnam in a joint venture with the Indian Oil and Natural Gas Corporation (ONGC) and PetroVietnam.[84] However, China has become the main energy claimant and the principal source of uncertainty for ASEAN. The China National Offshore Oil Corporation (CNOOC) and its subsidiary, PetroChina, are interested in expanding operations in the SCS through cooperative agreements with ASEAN.[85] However, when it comes to the management of inanimate resources, particularly oil and gas, the situation gets very complicated. An agreement between Japan and South Korea to jointly develop oil and gas in the East China Sea in 1974 generated severe protests from China. Recently, China and Japan have been fighting over the Chunxiao oil and gas field located just 5 km from Japan's unilaterally claimed middle line in the East China Sea. This dispute has been resolved partially in line with the UNCLOS Convention.

A report published by the *Washington Times* in 2005 stated that China is adopting a "string of pearls" strategy of bases and diplomatic ties which is to include a new naval base at the Pakistani port of Gwadar. The Chinese funded port is only 390 nm from the Hormuz Straits. In case of a disruption in the Straits of Malacca, oil imports could be diverted through there and then transported via the Gilgit region to western China.[86] The 2011 Pacific Energy Summit held in Jakarta, Indonesia, on February 21–23, featured the theme "Unlocking the Potential of Natural Gas in the Asia-Pacific." The summit explored the role of natural gas with regard to energy security and climate change in the region. Experts predicted that a Golden Age of gas in the Asia-Pacific region is on its way. In fact, unconventional gas production technology is providing access to vast new reserves of natural gas. At the same time, emerging liquefied natural gas (LNG) infrastructure in the region, rising production, and increased global availability have enabled natural gas to play a significant role in energy diversification efforts.

By 2020, Asia is expected to be the world's largest regional market for natural gas. Unprecedented growth is characteristic of the Asia-Pacific region today, with China at the forefront of rapid economic expansion followed by India. The International Energy Agency (IEA) projected that China will account for half of global oil demand growth in the next five years, while over the next 25 years, demand from Organization for Economic Co-operation and Development (OECD) countries such as the United States, Japan, and Europe will remain flat.[87] Despite various constraints, new regional pipeline developments have begun to take shape as the continental markets of Asia evolve. Beijing is enhancing its pipeline diplomacy initiatives to sponsor new major regional gas pipelines from Turkmenistan, Kazakhstan, and Myanmar.

The objective is to construct a large west-to-east domestic trunk-line gas pipe-line infrastructure to accommodate China's growing imports of LNG.[88] Huge advances in drilling technology and the growing interest of foreign compa-nies in exploring petroleum resources in this region have intensified disputes. Rich hydrocarbon deposits in Brunei and the Malaysian state of Sabah have also been discovered.[89] It is estimated that the SCS region, excluding the Paracels and Spratlys, has proven oil reserves of approximately 7.8 billion barrels and current oil production within the region is well over 1.9 million barrels per day.[90] In fact, total SCS production continues to grow as more and more oil wells in China, Malaysia, and Vietnam have become operational.[91] Beijing is even seriously considering creating a strategic petroleum reserve (SPR) because of its growing energy security initiatives. Chinese investment partners currently include: Eni, BP, ExxonMobil, Phillips Petroleum, Shell, Texaco, and Mitsubishi.[92]

China announced a plan to establish Xinjiang as the country's largest oil and gas production and storage base. By 2020, China National Petroleum Cor-poration (CNPC) aims to boost the province's hydrocarbon production capac-ity to 450 million barrels of oil equivalent.[93] However, since the 1990s, the Chinese petroleum strategy has also called for an active Chinese participation in international oil and gas exploration to secure a diversified supply structure. In 1992, China awarded the WananBei 21 oil exploration concession in the southwestern part of the Spratlys to the Crestone Energy Corporation based in Colorado. Since the majority of the concession area is located within Viet-nam's declared 200 nm EEZ, it led to severe protests by Vietnam.[94]

There has been increased exploration in China's onshore Junggar, Turpan-Hami, and Ordos Basins, although the Tarim Basin in northwestern China's Xinjiang Uygur Autonomous Region has been the main focus of new onshore oil prospects. Petro China reported that reserve additions in 2009 were 3.3 billion barrels of oil equivalent. China's national oil companies (NOCs) are investing to increase oil recovery rates at the country's mature oil fields. In fact, CNPC is utilizing natural gas supplies from the Daqing field for rein-jection purposes to fuel enhanced oil recovery (EOR) projects. CNPC hopes that EOR techniques will help to stabilize Daqing's oil output in the coming years. China's domestic demand for natural gas supplies is also increasing at the same time. This might put a competing claim on oil output from Daqing.[95]

Beyond energy per se, there are still other reasons for potential conflict in the SCS. First, as has been emphasized, is the overlapping claim by claim-ants, namely Brunei, China, Malaysia, the Philippines, Vietnam, and Taiwan pursuant to the EEZ concept as stated in article 55 of the 1982 UNCLOS? A second concern is the use of the high seas for military activities, including MSR by other states in the coastal states' EEZ. UNCLOS article 58 regards intelligence gathering as a part of the exercise of freedom of international navigation, and although such intelligence gathering is thus permitted, incidents, like that of the *Impeccable* in March 2009, still occur. A third source of friction concerns the Proliferation Security Initiative (PSI) announced by President Bush in 2003. According to this initiative, there will be increasing international cooperation to interdict shipments of weapons of mass destruction (WMD) and their related materials. However, the regional states objected to various aspects of the PSI and hence its application was at least controversial in the case of the SCS.[96] Finally, PSI accepted that freedom of navigation and stability in the SCS is equally important to the coastal states of the Southeast Asia as well as to the extra-regional powers.

Piracy and maritime terrorism have become yet another persistent threat and source of tension with regard to maritime security in the SCS region. The SCS has always been a haven for pirates. Thirty percent of piracy crimes occur in Indonesian waters.[97] The piracy issue has become a bone of contention between the countries in the region. In fact, suppressing piracy was often used as an excuse for naval buildups and naval deployments, thereby creating further suspicion and distrust in other countries. China has realized that regional cooperation is necessary to combat piracy in its adjacent seas and in that connection has signed the Joint Declaration on cooperation in the Field of Non-Traditional Security Issues with the ASEAN in November 2002.[98]

The term "core interest" has important significance when describing China's intentions in the SCS area. If the SCS issue is really a matter of "core interest" to China, which would place it on at par with other sovereignty issues such as Tibet and Taiwan, perhaps justifying military intervention in the region. A foreign ministry spokesperson did comment at a news conference that China has "indisputable sovereignty" over the Spratly Islands. But there have been no such statements concerning their position in the SCS as a whole. In fact, China has internal political disagreements regarding the SCS since they do not speak with precision about the SCS.[99] Some of their claims are not even officially documented. This further indicates that China's outward policy has been somewhat ambiguous with regard to any claim of total sovereignty over the area.

Nonetheless, the Chinese military (the People's Liberation Army or PLA) has declared that China has "indisputable sovereignty" over the SCS and this has naturally generated grave concern both in Washington and Asia. Countries have started to believe that China's policy is becoming more and more aggressive. China's navy has been demonstratively more aggressive at sea, seizing fishing boats, arresting sailors from other countries, and exchanging gunfire.[100] General MiZehnyu bluntly stated: "China must develop a strong sea power to protect and not yield a single inch of its three million square kilometers of ocean territory. China must 'build a new Chinese maritime great wall.'"[101]

WILL THERE BE MORE MISCALCULATIONS?

No global maritime power can ignore the SCS since all maritime traffic tra-
versing that sea passes between the Spratly and Paracel archipelagos. Hence,
the importance of sovereignty and strategic control over these groups of
islands is plainly apparent. As Mahan, as cited in Livezey, pointed out "sea
power consists in the first place of a proper navy and a proper fleet; but in
order to sustain a navy, we must have suitable places where a navy can be
protected and refurnished."[102] Sea power, it might be argued, is experiencing
a major revival today and thus it is clear why the SCS in general, and the
Spratly and Paracel Islands in particular, are strategically important. They
offer potential for a strong maritime presence as well as places to shelter and
reequip naval forces in the area. It seems that China is following its blue water
strategy both to increase prestige and to support pursuit of expanding national
interests, much as the United States did back in the early twentieth Century.

The SCS's growing strategic significance as well as increasing military
competition in the region guarantees that there will be more opportunities for
miscalculation. When the PLAN conduct further exercises and activities at
sea, the risks will rise. Research vessels will do their preparatory work, and
other militaries will step up surveillance, resulting in an increased number of
vessels in a limited space. The PLA is even developing new platforms and
capabilities to address still other objectives within the East and South China
Seas, and possibly even into the Indian Ocean.

Today, sea trade is so internationally intertwined that the disruption of
trade to one country will invariably bring dire economic consequences on
others. As Modelski and Thompson mention, command of the sea allows
its possessor to set the rules of the international order, provide security, and
prevent war.[103] Although an all-out war between the United States and China
in the foreseeable future is not very likely, and a global naval war is even
less likely, at some point there could be a struggle for control of the seas
somewhere in the vicinity ranging from the Yellow Sea down to the Straits
of Malacca. China's *Mahanian* navy may try to muscle out both the USN
and its bordering countries, and there is no end to this race. For example,
with China's expanding naval capabilities, Beijing's admirals have decided
to work more closely with other countries. China has even started to cooperate with the Japanese and Indian navies in patrolling against piracy off the
coast of Somalia. This patrol coordination policy was implemented in 2012.
Experts hope that such cooperation will have a positive normative effect
on civilian and military leadership. Beijing's new move to "go along to get
along" presents a picture of avoiding enmity and competition even while
expanding its military might abroad. However, matters may be different
with respect to China's perceived core interests in waters closer to China.

Reubel argues that if the Chinese could adopt the current US maritime strategy of "A Cooperative Strategy for 21st Century Sea Power" (CS21), then things would work well for all.[104] After all, as the U.S. Defense Secretary of State, Hagel stated that the SCS is the beating heart of the Asia-Pacific and a crossroads for the global economy.[105]

One plausible interpretation is that China is trying to dominate the entire area militarily by establishing a chain of outposts in the SCS region. New missile units outfitted at various locations in China could be used in a variety of non-Taiwan contingencies. Aerial-refueling programs and Airborne Early Warning and Control (AEW&C) will allow for extended air operations into the SCS.[106] At the same time, China is trying to use soft power through capacity-building assistance in a range of marine and environmental initiatives, such as Partnerships in Environmental Management for the Seas of East Asia (PEMSEA), the UNEP/GEF SCS project, and the Cooperative Mechanism for Navigational Safety and Environmental Protection in the Malacca and Singapore Straits. In sum, although China's official policy of "peaceful rise" recognizes the international values of peace, international order, and cooperation, that policy is becoming increasingly suspect.[107]

The next chapter discusses about the conflicts that took place in the SCS during the Cold War and the post-Cold War era.

NOTES

1. Rand Corporation, "The United States and Asia: Toward a New U.S. Strategy and Force Posture," Project Air Force Report (2001).

2. Tridib Chakraborti, "The Territorial Claims in South China Sea: Probing Persistent Uncertainties," in *Peoples Republic of China at Fifty: Politics, Economy and Foreign Relations*, ed. Arun Kumar Banerjee and Purushottam Bhattacharya (New Delhi: LancerPublication, 2001), 173.

3. David Rosenberg, "Governing The South China Sea: From Freedom of The Seas to Ocean Enclosure Movements," *Harvard Asia Quarterly* (Winter 2010).

4. Chakraborti, "The Territorial Claims in South China Sea," 178.

5. Li Jinming and Li Dexia, "The Dotted Line on the Chinese Map of the South China Sea: A Note," *Ocean Development and International Law* 34 (2003): 292.

6. Ibid.

7. Chin Yoon Chin, "Potential For Conflict in the Spratly Islands," Master's thesis (Naval Postgraduate School, Monterey, CA, 2003), 123.

8. Ibid.

9. Ibid.

10. Keyuan Zou, "Historic Rights in International Law and in China's Practice," *Ocean Development and International Law* 32, no. 2 (2001).

11. Ibid.

12. Ibid., 160.

13. Ibid.

14. Daniel Dzurek, "The Spratly Islands Dispute: Who's On First?" *International Boundaries Research Unit Maritime Briefing* 2, no. 1 (1996): 12.

15. Ministry of Foreign Affairs of the People's Republic of China, "China's Indisputable Sovereignty Over the Xisha and Nansha Islands," *Beijing Review*, January 30, 1980): 7.

16. Chakraborti, "The Territorial Claims in South China Sea," 178.

17. "Background Information on The Paracels and Spratlys," http://www.paracels.info/Sovereignty%20over%20the%20Paracel%20and%20Spratly%20Islands.pdf.

18. Ministry of Foreign Affairs, Socialist Republic of Vietnam, "The Hoang Sa and Truong Sa Archipelagos and International Law" (Hanoi, April 1988), 21.

19. Mark J. Valencia, Jon M. Van Dyke, and Noel A. Ludwig, *Sharing the Resources of the South China Sea* (Honolulu: University of Hawaii Press, 1999).

20. Dong Manh Nguyen, "Settlement of disputes under the 1982 United Nations Convention on the Law of the Sea: The case of the South China Sea dispute" (UN-Nippon Foundation, New York, December 2005): 9.

21. Ibid., 11.

22. Dzurek, "The Spratly Islands Dispute: Who's On First?" 4.

23. Ibid.

24. Ibid.

25. Esmond, D. Smith, "China's Aspirations in the Spratly Islands," *Contemporary Southeast Asia* 16, no. 3 (December 1994): 276.

26. David Hancox and Victor Prescott, "A Geographical Description of the Spratly Islands and an Account of Hydrographic Surveys amongst those Islands," *IBRU* 1, no. 6 (1995): 5.

27. Ministry of Foreign Affairs, Socialist Republic of Vietnam, "The Hoang Sa and Truong Sa Archipelagos and International Law," 22.

28. Michael Klare, *Resource Wars: The New Landscape of Global Conflict* (New York: Henry Holt and Company, LLC, 2001).

29. Valencia, Van Dyke, and Ludwig, *Sharing the Resources of the South China Sea.*

30. Mark J. Valencia, "The Spratly Islands: Dangerous Ground in the South China Sea," *The Pacific Review* 1, no. 4 (1998): 438.

31. Ibid., 434.

32. Ibid.

33. Valencia, Van Dyke, and Ludwig, *Sharing the Resources of the South China Sea.*

34. Carlyle Thayer, "The United States and Chinese Assertiveness in the South China Sea," *Security Challenges* 6, no. 2 (Winter 2010).

35. Ralph Cossa, ed. "Confidence Building Measures in the South China Sea," *Pacific Forum* SIS, no. 2-01 (August 2001).

36. David Rosenberg and Christopher Chung, "Maritime Security in the South China Sea: Coordinating Coastal and User State Priorities," *Ocean Development and International Law* 39 (2008): 51–52.

37. Rosenberg, "Governing The South China Sea."

38. Scott Snyder, "The SCS Dispute: Prospects for Preventive Diplomacy" (Special Report No. 18 of the United States Institute of Peace, 1996).

39. John Baker and David Wiencek, eds. *Cooperative Monitoring in the South China Sea: Satellite Imagery, Confidence Building Measures, and the Spratly Island Disputes* (Westport, CT: Praeger, 2002).

40. David Livingstone, "The Spratly Islands: A Regional Perspective," *Journal of the Washington Institute of China Studies* 1, no. 2 (Fall 2006).

41. Christopher Joyner, "The Spratly Islands Dispute: Legal Issues and Prospects for Diplomatic Accommodation," in *Cooperative Monitoring in the South China Sea: Satellite Imagery, Confidence Building Measures, and the Spratly Island Disputes*, ed. John Baker and David Wiencek (Westport, CT: Praeger, 2002), 19.

42. Information Office of the State Council of the People's Republic of China, "China's National Defense in 2008" (January 2009).

43. Carlyle Thayer, "The United States and Chinese Assertiveness in the South China Sea"; Ian Storey. "China's 'Malacca Dilemma'," *The Jamestown Foundation China Brief* 6, no. 8 (April 12, 2006).

44. Christopher Joyner, "The Spratly Islands Dispute in the South China Sea," 61.

45. Dzurek. "The Spratly Islands Dispute: Who's On First?"

46. Ibid., 19.

47. Ibid., 20.

48. Ibid.

49. Ibid., 20.

50. Ibid., 20-21.

51. Valencia, Van Dyke, and Ludwig, *Sharing the Resources of the South China Sea*, 38.

52. Ibid.

53. Ibid., 19.

54. Klare, *Resource Wars*, 109.

55. Pooja Stanslas, "The Spratly Dilemma: External powers and Dispute Resolution Mechanisms," *Biuletyn Opinie* 34 (November 2, 2010), 3.

56. The UNEP Shelf Program (UNEP/GRID-Arendal) began in 2003 following a resolution of the UN General Assembly calling on UNEP's GRID network to coordinate work on marine data related to article 76 of the United Nations Convention on the Law of the Sea. For further information, http://www.continentalshelf.org/about/1143.aspx.

57. Nguyen, "Settlement of Disputes under the 1982 United Nations Convention on the Law of the Sea," 2.

58. United Nations Convention on the Law of the Sea, Montego Bay, December 10, 1982, entered into force November 10, 1994, 1833 UNTS 397, arts. 2 & 3, available at http://www.un.org/Depts/los/convention_agreements/texts/unclos/closindx.htm.

59. Ibid.

60. Ibid.

61. United Nations Convention on the Law of the Sea, Montego Bay, December 10, 1982, entered into force November 10, 1994, 1833 UNTS 397, arts. 2 & 3, Part v. http://www.un.org/Depts/los/convention_agreements/texts/unclos/closindx.htm.

62. http://www.un.org/depts/los/convention_agreements/texts/unclos/part5.htm.

63. Sam Bateman, "UNCLOS and Its Limitations as the Foundation for a Regional Maritime Regime" (Working Paper No. 111, Institute of Defense and Strategic Studies, Singapore, 2006).

64. Daniel Coulter, "South China Sea Fisheries: Countdown to Calamity," *Contemporary Southeast Asia* 17, no. 4 (March 1996), 378.

65. Geographically disadvantaged states are the coastal states, including states bordering enclosed or semi-enclosed seas. Their geographical situation makes them dependent upon the exploitation of the living resources of the exclusive economic zones of other states in the subregion or region for adequate supplies of fish for the nutritional purposes of their populations and coastal states that can claim no exclusive economic zones of their own.

66. For further details, see the 1982 UNCLOS at http://www.un.org/Depts/los/convention_agreements/texts/unclos/closindx.htm;http://www.un.org/Depts/los/convention_agreements/texts/unclos/unclos_e.pdf

67. John Prescott, The Maritime Political Boundaries of the World (New York: Methuen, 1985), 377.

68. Ralf Emmers, "Introduction: The South China Sea: Towards a Cooperative Management Regime," in *Security and International Politics in the South China Sea: Towards a Co-operative Management Regime*, eds. Sam Bateman and Ralf Emmers (London: Routledge, 2009).

69. Nguyen, "Settlement of disputes under the 1982 United Nations Convention on the Law of the Sea"; Lowell Bautista, "Thinking Outside the Box: The South China Sea Issue and the United Nations Convention on the Law of the Sea: (Options, Limitations and Prospects)," Philippines Law Journal 81 (2006).

70. Gerald Segal and Richard Yang, eds. *Chinese Economic Reform: The Impact on Security* (London: Routledge, 1996), 142.

71. Snildal Knut, "Petroleum in the South China Sea—a Chinese National Interest?" Thesis, Department of Political Science (University of Oslo, June 2000).

72. Robert Frost used this phrase in the blank verse poem "Mending Wall" published in 1914.

73. A baseline is a legal construct, a boundary line that determines where a state's maritime sovereignty and jurisdiction begins and ends. In fact, baselines determine all areas of maritime jurisdiction. This creates a demarcation between areas where a state has no rights and those where a state does enjoy rights. The default baseline under UNCLOS is known as the normal baseline. According to article 5 of UNCLOS, a normal baseline is drawn at the low water line. Waters on the landward side of a baseline are considered a state's internal waters. However, in some situations it is either impractical or uneconomical to draw a normal baseline. In such cases, straight baselines are used. The first guidelines for drawing straight baselines arose out of one of the most famous and contentious cases in international law—the 1951 Anglo-Norwegian Fisheries Case. For further information, see http://www.aggregat456.com/2010/02/baselines-straight-and-normal.html.

74. John Prescott, "Straight and Archipelagic Baselines," in *Maritime Boundaries and Ocean Resources*, ed. Gerald Blake (Lanham, MD: Rowman & Littlefield Publishers, 1985), 187.

75. Thayer, "The United States and Chinese Assertiveness in the South China Sea," 73–74.

76. Ibid.

77. Economist, "China's assertiveness at sea- Choppy waters East and south, China makes a splash," January 21, 2010, http://www.economist.com/node/15331153

78. Nguyen, "Settlement of disputes under the 1982 United Nations Convention on the Law of the Sea."

79. Ibid.

80. Keyuan Zou, "Can China Respect The Law Of The Seas?: An Assessment Of Maritime Agreements Between China And Its Neighbors," *Harvard Asia Quarterly* (Winter 2010).

81. Chin, "Potential For Conflict in the Spratly Islands," 32.

82. Nguyen, "Settlement of Disputes under the 1982 United Nations Convention on the Law of the Sea."

83. Ibid.

84. Nong Hong, "Chinese Perceptions of the SCS Dispute," *Geopolitics of Energy* 30, no. 6 (June 2008).

85. Leszek Buszynski and Iskandar Sazlan, "Maritime Claims and Energy Cooperation in the South China Sea," *Contemporary Southeast Asia* 29, no. 1 (2007).

86. Bill Gertz, "China Builds Up Strategic Sea Lanes," *Washington Times*, January 17, 2005, http://www.washingtontimes.com/news/2005/jan/17/20050117-115550-1929r/; Emmanuel Karagiannis, "China's Pipeline Diplomacy: Assessing The Threat of Low-Intensity Conflicts," *Harvard Asia Quarterly* (Winter 2010).

87. National Bureau of Asian Research, "Unlocking the Potential of Natural Gas in the Asia-Pacific" (Pacific Energy Summit, 2011), http://www.nbr.org/downloads/pdfs/ETA/PES2011_summitreport.pdf

88. Mikkal E. Herberg, "Natural Gas in Asia: History and Prospects" (The National Bureau of Asian Research, Pacific Energy Summit, 2011).

89. Stanslas, "The Spratly Dilemma," 4.

90. U.S. Energy Information Administration, "China: Country Analysis Brief," September 4, 2012, http://www.eia.gov/countries/analysisbriefs/China/china.pdf.

91. U.S. Energy Information Administration, "South China Sea," Last modified February 7, 2013, http://www.eia.gov/countries/analysisbriefs/South_China_Sea/south_china_sea.pdf

92. U.S. Energy Information Administration, "China: Country Analysis Brief."

93. Ibid.

94. Knut, Petroleum in the South China Sea—a Chinese National Interest?

95. See U.S. Energy Information Administration, "China: Country Analysis Brief."

96. Nik Ramli, "Troubled Waters in the South China Sea," Biuletyn Opinie, April 13, 2010, http://www.kwasniewskialeksander.eu/attachments/BIULETYN_OPINIE_FAE_Troubled_Waters_in_the_South_China_Sea.pdf.

97. Catherine Zara Raymond, "Piracy and Armed Robbery in the Malacca Strait: A Problem Solved?" *Naval War College Review* 62, no. 3 (2009): 36.

98. Zou, "Historic Rights in International Law and in China's Practice."

99. Ibid.

100. John Promfret, "Beijing Claims 'Indisputable Sovereignty' over South China," *Washington Post*, July 31, 2010, http://www.washingtonpost.com/wp-dyn/content/article/2010/07/30/AR2010073005664.html.

101. Jing-Dong Yuan, "Asia-Pacific Security: China's Conditional Multilateralism and Great Power Entente" (Strategic Studies Institute, US Army War College, 2000), 18.

102. William E. Livezey, *Mahan on Sea Power* (Norman, OK: University of Oklahoma Press, 1981), 181.

103. George Modelski and William R. Thompson, *Seapower in Global Politics, 1494–1993* (Seattle, WA: University of Washington Press, 1988).

104. The three maritime forces of the United States—the Navy, Marine Corps, and Coast Guard have come together and created a unified maritime strategy, which integrates sea power with other elements of national power. It discusses how sea power will work around the world and protect our life. For details, see Robert C. Reubel, "Is China the Real Mahanian Maritime Power of the 21st Century?" Information Dissemination: The Intersection of Maritime Strategy and Strategic Communications, June 12, 2012, http://www.informationdissemination.net/2012/06/is-china-real-mahanian-maritime-power.html; see also Washington Post, "China's navy engaging in unprecedented coordination with India, Japan on anti-piracy patrols," July 3, 2012.

105. Jim Garamone, U.S. Will Continue to Lead in 21st Century, American Forces Press Service | May 31, 2014. http://iipdigital.usembassy.gov/st/english/article/2014/05/20140531300646.html#axzz4CKmGc3ND

106. William E. Livezey, *Mahan on Sea Power*.

107. Bonnie Glaser and Evan Medeiros, "The Changing Ecology of Foreign Policy-Making in China: The Ascension and Demise of the Theory of 'Peaceful Rise'," *China Quarterly* 190 (2007).

Chapter 3

Clashes in the South China Sea

War is a game of deception. Therefore, feign incapability when in fact capable; feign inactivity when ready to strike; appear to be far away when actually nearby, and vice versa.

—Sun Tzu

Southeast Asian states are highly sovereignty sensitive, and this sensitivity has made the principle of nonintervention the bedrock of foreign policy and interregional state relations. Seas are a central concern for Southeast Asian countries,[1] so it is hardly surprising that the countries in the region are strongly nationalistic in asserting and protecting their claims. Mark Valencia comments, "Indeed, when countries in Asia think maritime, they think first and foremost about boundary disputes, not protection of the deteriorating marine environment or management of dwindling fisheries," and he further states that, "[i] t is these perceptions that must change."[2] Geoffrey Till once observed that "claims to the sovereignty of islands can be important symbolically, perhaps especially in times of national difficulty."[3]

In fact, the sovereignty issues in the SCS are extremely complex and as Ian Townsend-Gault comments, "too much ink has been spilled on that issue without making progress."[4] The uneasiness of the Philippines over the joint maritime seismic undertaking (JMSU), as it seemed to weaken Philippine sovereignty claims, is a clear manifestation of nationalism.[5] The initial agreement was signed by China and the Philippines in 2004 to jointly explore oil in the SCS, and Vietnam later joined in 2005. The JMSU was initially regarded as a breakthrough and watershed for diplomacy. It also indicated a growing level of trust and confidence among claimants to pursue peaceful options. However, this changed after Vietnam joined. Since the JMSU site covered about 80 percent of the Philippines' exclusive economic zone (EEZ), the agreement implied that the Philippines "acknowledged the area involved as disputed."[6]

The SCS constitutes the first line of defense for the littoral states of Southeast Asia.[7] As Singapore's deputy prime minister stated, individual state action is not enough; the oceans are indivisible and maritime security threats do not respect boundaries.[8] As will be explained further in this chapter, despite—or perhaps because of—intensifying disputes, maritime security cooperation in Southeast Asia appears to be developing more quickly than in the preceding decade.[9] A number of clashes have occurred over the control of specific islands and reefs within the SCS. According to Tonnesson, the history of the disputes in the SCS can be understood by focusing on the nationalist perspective, by creating a chronology of conflicting claims to sovereignty, or by examining a history of international events and analyzing trends based on the changes in the international system.[10] This chapter utilizes all three of these approaches and focuses mainly on disputes that arose or became more salient during the Cold War (1945–1992) and the post-Cold War era (1993–present). Table 3.1 summarizes significant events that took place in this region since the twelfth century and even continues to the present.

MILITARY ENGAGEMENTS DURING THE COLD WAR PERIOD

The question of sovereignty over the Spratly Islands first arose when foreign powers like Britain and France started exerting their influence in the 1800s. Before that, Chinese ships dominated trade in the SCS from the twelfth to mid-fifteenth century. In fact, Chinese naval and commercial shipping went through a period of intense expansion during the fourteenth to early fifteenth century.[11] Later, when the emperor ordered an end to the building of ocean-going ships, this opened new possibilities for other maritime nations like the Portuguese, who were followed by the Dutch, to explore opportunities for expanding trade. The Dutch for example, dominated the lucrative spice trade during the seventeenth century. However, during the eighteenth and nineteenth centuries, the Vietnamese Nguyen Kings, Gia Long (1802–1820), and later Minh Mang (1820-47), pursued an active maritime policy claiming sovereignty to the Paracels.[12]

But there was a new phase when the Europeans started a systematic survey of the Spratlys and Paracels. Most of the areas surrounding the SCS were made into British, French, and Spanish colonies, and hence treaties were agreed to separate them from each other. The British established Singapore as a port city, launched the Opium War (1839–1842), acquired Hong Kong, and established protectorates in Malaya and northern Borneo. The French colonized the whole of Indochina (Vietnam, Cambodia, and Laos) from 1863 to 1884 and leased a territory on the Liaozhou peninsula.[13] Although the monarchies in China, Japan, and Thailand were not fully subjugated, they were forced to open themselves up. Their governments had to learn new techniques of mapping and demarcating land borders, delineating territorial waters, planting flags, and establishing sovereignty markers on islands.[14] Toward the end of the nineteenth century, Britain, France, Japan, and China all advanced competing claims to the Spratlys.[15] In 1870, a group of merchants in northern Borneo wanted to exploit bird dung used as fertilizer on the Spratly Islands and the Amboyna Cay. Consequently, the British Crown formally claimed these two islands in 1877. The Sino-French Treaty of 1887 established a land boundary between China and French Indochina, and this border remained contested for much of the twentieth century.[16] From this point forward until 1933, the Spratly Islands and Amboyna Cay were regularly included in the British colonial list, though little was done to exploit them or sustain the British sovereignty claim.[17] Although the Paracels occupied a strategic position, neither Britain nor France took any initiatives to claim the archipelago before the 1930s. In the first decades of the twentieth century, only the Chinese empire displayed an interest in the Paracels until China fell apart and suffered a series of civil wars. However, from 1894–1895, Japan destroyed the Chinese navy and established a presence in the SCS through the annexation of Taiwan.[18]

The fear of Japanese expansion led France to gain an interest both in the Spratlys and the Paracels.[19] In 1930–1933, France claimed the Spratlys for itself and occupied some of them. In 1938, France established what was designed to be a permanent presence in the Paracels, which were at this point also claimed on behalf of the protectorate of Annam (today's central Vietnam).[20] According to France, the stationing of a French garrison in the Paracels had a defensive purpose. Although Britain did not oppose French action, Britain did not abandon its own 1877 claim to the Spratly Islands and Amboyna Cay. Before occupying Hainan in 1939, Japan established a military presence both in the Paracels and the Spratlys. Toward the end of World War II, the most active claimant was the ROC (the government of Chiang Kai-shek), which sent naval expeditions both to the Paracels and the Spratlys in 1945–1946. As previously mentioned, China even established a "permanent" presence on both Woody Island and Itu Aba.

In 1947–1948, Chiang Kai-shek's government published the dotted U-shaped line map encompassing virtually all of the SCS (as previously discussed in chapter 2). However, after Chiang Kai-shek's government

Table 3.1 Key Events and Actors in Southeast Asia from the Twelfth Century to the Present

Period	Actors Involved	Key Events
Twelfth to mid-fifteenth century	China	Chinese ships dominated trade
Seventeenth century	Dutch	Dominated spice trade
Eighteenth and nineteenth centuries	Vietnamese Nguyen Kings	Pursued an active maritime policy claiming sovereignty to the Paracels
Colonial Period	European powers	The British Crown claimed two islands (1877)
World War I and World War II	France, Japan, and China	France claimed the Spratlys (1930–1933); Japan occupied Hainan (1939); Chiang Kai-shek's government published the dotted U-shaped map; China established a permanent presence on the Woody Island and Itu Aba respectively, Japan occupies Spratlys (1934–1944).
Cold War	France, Japan, and Philippines	The Philippines (1946) and Vietnam (1950) emerged as the first decolonized states; Peace conference in San Francisco (1951); Philippines proclaimed the area as Kalayaan; Japan renounces all rights to Spratly Islands (1951).
1974	China-Vietnam	Chinese invasion of the Paracels in 1974; airship built in the Woody island; Soviet Union started building up air and naval facilities in the Cam Ranh Bay leading to small clashes between 1979 and 1982.
1988	China-Vietnam	Fiery Cross Reef Incident: Construction of a Chinese base at Fiery Cross Reef; China continued occupying few other reefs resulting in an armed clash at Johnson reef on March 14, 1988; Vietnam and China normalized their diplomatic relationship in November 1991. Vietnam adds 15 features to claim while PRC seizes 6 isles.
Post-Cold War/ 1992	China-Vietnam	Dispute between China and Vietnam drilling oil in the Gulf of Tonkin; By the end of 2008, the two countries concluded the Gulf of Tonkin agreement; ASEAN Declaration on the South China Sea concerning regional security was promulgated (1992); China occupies Da Lac Reef (July 1992).

Year	Parties	Event
1995	China-Philippines	Mischief Reef Incident: Building of a base, and the occupation of the Mischief Reef by China.
1995	China-Malaysia	First military clash took place with no serious consequences.
1995	Vietnam-Taiwan	Taiwanese artillery fired on the Vietnamese supply ship.
1996–1997	China-Philippines	90-minute gun battle with a Philippine navy gunboat near Campones Island; and the Philippine navy ordered a Chinese speedboat and two fishing boats to leave the Scarborough Shoal in April.
2001	China-U.S.	USNS Bowditch; ASEAN and China sign Free Trade Agreement.
2001	China-U.S.	EP-3 Incident.
2009	China-U.S.	USNS Impeccable.
2009	China-U.S.	USNS Victorious.
2009	China-Philippines	Philippines Baseline Bill.
2009	China-Vietnam	Fight over a multibillion dollar Sino-Vietnam development of bauxite reserves in Vietnam's Central Highlands.
2010	China-U.S.	China communicated to the U.S. that the South China Sea is "an area of core interest that is as non-negotiable."
2011	China-India	China objected to India's naval presence (INS Airavat) and oil exploration with Vietnam.
2011	China-Vietnam	Naval ships from China attacked and cut the cable of Vietnamese oil exploration ship.
2011–2012	China-Philippines	Fight over the Scarborough Shoal.
2012	China-Taiwan	Taiwan rejected a pan-Chinese approach of coordinating with the PRC regarding claims to the South China Sea.
2013	China-Philippines	China rejected Philippines proposal to take the SCS dispute to the ICJ.
2014	China-Vietnam	Armed clashes took place in the Vietnam coast.
2014	China-Philippines	Armed clashes in the South China Sea.
2015	China-Philippines	Armed clashes in the Scarborough Shoal.

Source: Compiled by author; Tønnesson, "The History of the Dispute," 6.

fled to Taiwan, Itu Aba and Woody Island, as well as the other Spratly and
Paracel Islands, remained unoccupied for some time.[21] With the onset of the
Cold War, the Philippines (1946) and Vietnam (1950) emerged as the first
decolonized states. At the 1951 peace conference held in San Francisco,
Japan formally abandoned its claims to Hainan, Taiwan, and all other islands
in the SCS. However, the treaty did not state to whom the other islands were
ceded until the Philippines proclaimed the area as Kalayaan or Freedomland,
in 1956.[22]

VIETNAM AND CHINA

This bilateral dispute over the control of the Paracel and Spratly archipelagos dates back to the Vietnam War. In 1973, four U.S. oil companies signed
contracts with the South Vietnamese government of President Nguyen Thieu
and, with the oil crisis looming, began exploration. Before 1974, the East
Paracel islands were occupied by the People's Republic of China, while the
West Paracel islands were occupied by South Vietnam. The Chinese showed
renewed interest in the Paracels by sending fishing fleets with navy escorts
in early January 1974. South Vietnam's resistance to this move led to severe
military clashes and thus set the stage for China to occupy three Paracel
islands in the Crescent group.

Vietnam's claim to the islands was based on two arguments. First, Vietnam
had exercised historical dominion and control over the Spratly islands dating
back to 1650–1653. Second, the islands are located within Vietnam's continental shelf.[23] China feared the close contact between the North Vietnam and
the Soviet Union. Therefore, Chinese occupation of part of the Paracels was
regarded by China as a means to counter a growing Soviet naval presence
in the SCS region. It is important to note that the United States maintained
a neutral position throughout the conflict over the Paracels. Although North
Vietnam supported the Chinese claim of control, Taiwan and Philippines
strongly protested. China strengthened its administrative control over the
Paracels in the late 1970s.

On May 12, 1977, Vietnam declared sovereignty over both the Spratlys
and the newly Chinese-occupied Paracel Islands within a 200-mile EEZ.[24] As
a reaction to Vietnam's declaration, China's foreign minister, Huang Hua,
abruptly declared, "When the time comes, China will retrieve those islands,"
and further stated that, "[t] here will be no need then to negotiate at all."[25]
Vietnam did not relinquish its claims to either island group in the Spratlys
or the small airstrip located there. Vietnam's main garrison was situated on
Sin Cowe Island and fortified with heavy artillery and anti-aircraft guns.[26] A
Paracel maritime police district was also set up in 1978 by China along with

infrastructural construction by the Chinese government. China built an airstrip on Woody Island in 1978 and air service to Hainan began in August 1979.

In January 1980, the Chinese PLAN navigation Safety Department issued a navigational chart of the Paracels. Lighthouses were also constructed on Bombay Reef on the southeast limit of the Paracel group and on the north reef lying to the northwest limit. This was done because both these points were regarded as major international commercial passageways. A new harbor was even constructed on Triton Island by the PLAN in 1982. Beijing also entered in a "battle of documents" with Hanoi to substantiate its claim to ownership of Paracels and Spratlys.[27] In fact, the signing of the Treaty of Friendship and Cooperation between Vietnam and Soviet Union changed the course of disputes in the SCS region. The Soviet Union started strengthening air and naval facilities in the Cam Ranh Bay, and this led to the outbreak of small clashes between China and Vietnam in the Paracel Islands between 1979 and 1982. The worst dispute to that date took place in 1979 when 24 Vietnamese fishermen were arrested by the Chinese fleet and kept in custody for over one year.[28] Once the Paracels came firmly in their hands, China ventured further to the Spratlys in the Bach Ho field area. This area was considered to be the largest and most productive by Vietnam, which was first developed by the joint venture Vietsovpetro. Established with the Soviet Union in 1981, it later involved a cooperation agreement between PetroVietnam and Russia's Zarubezhneft.

Beijing was accused of a serious violation in the SCS by Hanoi, which thought that the former was trying to claim its ownership of the whole sea and turn it into its "home pond." This incident took place 120 nms off the coast of Phu Yen province in south-central Vietnam, claimed by both China and Vietnam. PetroVietnam accused China of sabotaging Vietnamese oil exploration vessels. Vietnam stated that while they were conducting seismic survey and drilling operations, China flew airplanes over to monitor activity. PetroVietnam was working with a number of large international oil companies, including ExxonMobil and Chevron, to explore oil and gas assets in SCS waters claimed by Vietnam. China's next move came in May 1992 when Beijing announced the signing of an agreement between the Chinese National Offshore Oil Corporation and Crestone Energy Corporation of Denver to explore and develop oil in the 9,700 square mile Wanan B8i-21 Block (WAB-21) in the Vanguard Bank area of western Spratly.[29] Vietnam strongly protested this move and urged China to void the Crestone contract, as the exploration was located on their continental shelf area.[30] This was Beijing's first concession to a foreign company and instigated further complications in the SCS region, including renewed tension with Vietnam. The situation became worse when PetroVietnam and the Vietnamese State Oil Corporation began drilling in Crestone's concession area.[31]

THE FIERY CROSS REEF INCIDENT

In 1984, the Chinese navy conducted a major naval exercise in the Spratlys that involved the circumnavigation of islands occupied by Vietnam and two more exercises were conducted in 1986 as far as James Shoal. This meant that Beijing was becoming capable enough to operate militarily even when far away from home.[32] In late 1987, China announced its intention of setting up a number of observation stations in the Spratlys to conduct a comprehensive global oceanic survey, as requested by the United Nations Educational, Scientific and Cultural Organization (UNESCO) at the 14th Annual Intergovernmental UNESCO Conference held in March 1987. In April and May 1987, the Chinese Academy of Sciences and the State Oceanic Bureau dispatched ships to investigate the possibility of establishing an observation station on one of the several uninhabited islands, or shoals, under a UNESCO plan. After various investigations were completed by the Chinese Academy of Sciences and the State Oceanic Bureau, it was decided that Fiery Cross[33] was the most suitable location.[34] Table 3.2 shows the geographic coordinates of Fiery Cross Reef.[35]

Construction of a Chinese base at Fiery Cross Reef started on March 14, 1988, and in August the construction was completed. Vietnamese forces tried to disrupt the construction work, which led to an armed battle. Seventy-five Vietnamese personnel were either killed or were reported missing, and three Vietnamese ships were set ablaze. Chinese casualties were apparently minor. The battle lasted for about 28 minutes.[36] Vietnam reported that three Chinese warships landed troops on Fiery Cross Reef and planted China's flag. When they were asked to leave, the Chinese troops opened fire. Vietnam declared that, "China was trying to seize sole control of the South China Sea, dominate this international lifeline, replace the United States navy in the region, hinder the soviet navy's navigation, apply political pressure on the Southeast Asian countries, build a military springboard in the region, seize territory, and exploit and plunder maritime resources."[37] However, China rejected this charge and warned:

Table 3.2   Geographic Coordinates of Fiery Cross Reef

Source	Latitude (N)	Longitude (E)
A	9 Degree 33′ 00″	112 Degree 53′ 00″
B	9 Degree 38	112 Degree 57′
C	9 Degree 32′ 30″	112 Degree 54′ 00″
D	9 Degree 42′	112 Degree 54′
E	9 Degree 33′ 02″	112 Degree 53′ 34″

Daniel Dzurek. "The Spratly Islands Dispute: Who's On First?" *International Boundaries Research Unit Maritime Briefing* 2, no. 1 (1996).

Vietnam has no right to interfere with Chinese vessels patrolling their territorial waters. It is Vietnam that has occupied illegally islands and reefs in China's Nansha islands. If the Vietnamese side ignores the consistent stand of the Chinese government and hinders our legitimate activities in these areas, it will have to bear the responsibility and the consequences.[38]

The Chinese version of the story was that a Chinese survey team landed on Fiery Cross Reef to set up an observation post. Three Vietnamese ships arrived and landed troops on the reef. When the Chinese asked them to leave, the Vietnamese opened fire. Hence, in retaliation, the Chinese ships had to fire.[39] On March 23, 1988, Vietnam offered to open talks on the Spratly dispute, an overture that was rejected by China. In response to what later developed into a public relations disaster, China agreed to negotiate with Vietnam and demanded the withdrawal of Vietnamese forces in May 1988. But China sent more ships to the islands and started occupying additional reefs, all the while warning Vietnam of possible military confrontation. China even warned Vietnam of another battle. Meanwhile, Hanoi occupied four more islets. China too continued occupying a few other reefs, which resulted in an armed clash at Johnson Reef in 1988. However, none of the parties regarded themselves as having initiated this conflict.[40] China sank three Vietnamese transport ships killing 72 seamen and taking nine prisoners. Shortly after the armed clash with China, the Vietnamese defense minister reportedly started visiting the Spratly Islands. Chinese Foreign Minister, QianQichen, defended China's actions by saying that China was only conducting a scientific and peaceful survey in the Nansha Islands. UNESCO, however, denied this claim. QianQichen promised that there would be no war in that area if Vietnam would stop occupying islands and reefs and withdraw all its troops. Meanwhile, Vietnam tried to garner the support for the Non-Aligned Movement (NAM)[41] at the United Nations (UN) to condemn this action, but failed.[42] In November 1988, Vietnam reported that a Chinese destroyer had fired on one of its ships, but China denied the incident. In August 1989, Vietnam started building facilities on Bombay Castle on Rifleman Bank, Vanguard Bank, and Prince of Wales Bank, thereby bringing 24 islets and reefs under its control.[43] Meanwhile, Soviet naval ships stayed out of the conflict as the U.S. 7th Fleet had done in 1974.[44]

Though not directly involved in the clash near the Fiery Cross Reef, other claimants reacted vigorously. Taiwan reacted by reasserting its sovereignty and re-supplying its garrison on Itu Aba. On March 17, 1988, the Philippines reacted to the China–Vietnam clash by warning both nations not to interfere in Kalayaan. In April of the same year, a Philippine delegation even visited Hanoi and reached an agreement not to use force in settling disputes. The following February, Malaysia's Deputy Foreign Minister stated,

The islands and atolls are under Malaysian sovereignty, and Malaysia has in the past reaffirmed its jurisdiction. . . . They are within Malaysia's continental shelf area and Malaysia's sovereignty over them has been officially declared through the new Map of Malaysia, published on December 21st, 1979. . . . The claim is in line with the Geneva Convention of 1958 pertaining to territorial waters and continental shelf boundaries, and the UN Convention on the Law of the Sea, as well as other international practices.[45]

In sum, the 1988 conflict bore some resemblance to the 1974 war insofar as China once again proved its military capability in the SCS region. Subsequently, for some years, the bilateral relationship between Vietnam and China appeared to improve. The two countries normalized their diplomatic relationship in November 1991.[46] At the end of 2008, the two countries finally signed the Gulf of Tonkin agreement, which defined a shared maritime area between China and Vietnam. This established a maritime boundary of approximately 500 km. The line has 21 geographic points, of which points 1 to 9 divide the territorial seas and points 9 to 21 delimit the EEZs and continental shelves of the two countries in the Gulf of Tonkin. This agreement seemed to promise a new era of maritime cooperation between the two parties.

China's strategic thinking toward Southeast Asia shifted from a land-based strategy in the Cold War to a sea-centered strategy in the post-Cold War era.[47] China's rapid economic growth along with the economic success of the ASEAN Newly Industrialized Economies (NIEs), including those of Malaysia, Indonesia, Thailand, Singapore, and the Philippines, bolstered trade and investment relations between China and Southeast Asian countries. The SCS became strategically more important for China as a link to Southeast Asian countries in terms of trade, investment, and communication. Hence, China never wanted to lose the sympathy of ASEAN.[48] During a visit to Singapore in 1990, Chinese Premier Li Peng said that the SCS conflict should be frozen and the exploitation of the natural resources should be managed by joint ventures until a peaceful solution could be reached. Li further explained that the territorial sovereignty of China could not be questioned; rather, joint venture cooperation should be initiated to enhance regional cooperation.[49]

A workshop held in Bandung, Indonesia, in 1991 was sponsored by the Indonesians to resolve their differences peacefully. However, China's move to acquire aerial-refueling technology and its decision to purchase an aircraft carrier from the Ukraine seemed inconsistent with the spirit of the agreement.[50] Furthermore, in 1992, the Standing Committee of the National People's Congress formally proclaimed Chinese sovereignty over the entire Spratly archipelago.[51] The situation continued to worsen when Chinese troops were deployed to erect a sovereignty marker on the Vietnamese-claimed Da Lac Reef, which was located close to the Crestone energy concession.[52]

Following Beijing's moves in 1992, ASEAN publicized its formal declaration known as the "ASEAN Declaration on the South China Sea" concerning regional security. Although China pledged to honor this declaration, Chinese intentions and actions remained a matter of concern. Appendix 3 summarizes the 1992 ASEAN Declaration.

A number of other minor clashes took place in the SCS in the post-Cold War period. The first one took place between China and Vietnam in 1992 when Vietnam accused Beijing of drilling oil in the Gulf of Tonkin. China reacted by seizing 20 Vietnamese cargo ships that were transporting goods from Hong Kong. The second clash between them took place in 1994. Both these countries were otherwise engaged in naval confrontations within territorial waters claimed by Vietnam over oil exploration blocks 133, 134 and 135. China also claimed the same area as part of their (WAB-21) block.[53]

MALAYSIA AND CHINA

In September 1991, China accused Malaysia of infringing on its territorial rights in the Spratlys after Kuala Lumpur decided to build an airstrip on TerumbuLayang-Layang in 1983. This military step was severely protested by both Vietnam[54] and China, and the latter claimed indisputable sovereignty over the reef it named Danwan. This also demonstrated that Kuala Lumpur was serious about defending its territorial claims, which included Amboyna Cay occupied by Vietnam since 1978. Malaysia's decision to increase its power in the region and to use force to resist aggression if necessary gave the island of Luban new strategic importance for securing sea-lanes between Peninsula Malaysia and Sarawak and Sabah. Its importance was even clearer after the conceding of the 91 square-mile island by the Sabah state to the central Malaysian government as a federal territory in 1984.[55]

Malaysia also had maritime disputes with the Philippines regarding the Swallow Reef and with Brunei regarding the Louisa Reef. Apart from Malaysia and the Philippines, no other ASEAN member states have had any major claims on the disputed islands of the SCS. However, in 1992, China reacted against an agreement signed by Vietnam and Malaysia to jointly develop any economic opportunity that might arise in the Spratlys.[56] That same year, China conducted an inspection in the Spratlys. The ship, after crossing through the eastern Spratlys, landed at James Shoal and placed "seven sovereignty" plates before returning to Hainan. By this time, China occupied nine islets in the Spratlys, including the Fiery Cross, SubiCuarteron, Johnson, Gaven, Eldad, and Dongmen reefs.[57] Finally in February 1992, the National People's Congress of China passed the "Law of the People's Republic of China on the Territorial Sea and Contiguous Zone," which laid down China's exclusive claim over the entirety of the Spratly Islands. The law further authorized the Chinese navy to evict trespassers by force.[58] This sudden declaration alarmed many ASEAN member countries.

The Philippines felt particularly vulnerable because of the U.S. withdrawal from its base and uncertainty about Washington's defense commitment to Manila in the Spratlys. Therefore, the Manila Declaration was initiated to resolve the sovereignty and jurisdictional issues in the Spratlys without resort to force. This Declaration represented one of the most remarkable demonstrations of political solidarity among the ASEAN member states on strategic issues of common concern. Vietnam by then had claimed 15 islands and reefs in the Spratlys and made clear that the nation's claims in both the Paracels and the Spratlys were mainly based on national security interests as well as on natural resources. Meanwhile, the Chairman of the Council of Ministers Continental Shelf Committee commented in an interview with the *Far Eastern Economic Review* that Vietnam had occupied 21 points including nine islands and he added that there were several thousand Vietnamese construction workers, scientists, and hydrological staff working in this area.[59] Malaysia was also in dispute with Indonesia over two small islands, Sipadan and Ligitan, in the Sulawesi Strait between Sabah and the Indonesian province of Kalimantan.[60]

MILITARY ENGAGEMENTS DURING THE POST–COLD WAR PERIOD

Since the end of the Cold War, China has reportedly tried to assure ASEAN that its military modernization was essentially meant for self-defense and not to "fill the power vacuum" either now or in the future. As a positive gesture, China entered into diplomatic relations with Indonesia, Singapore, and other ASEAN countries, but this move was insufficient to eradicate regional apprehension about Beijing's military modernization. In fact, this apprehension seemed entirely justified after the occupation of Mischief Reef by China in February 1995. Table 3.3 shows the major garrisoned islands in the Spratlys.

PHILIPPINES AND CHINA

The conflict between China and the Philippines had been latent from 1971 until 1994, when the Mischief Reef incident took place. Mischief Reef is located within Philippine waters and within its EEZ extending 200 nms from its coast. Mischief Reef is submerged at high tide and has little value. However, its occupation by China and the proceeding construction of facilities

Table 3.3 Major Garrisoned Islands in the Spratlys

Malaysian/ Standard Name	Chinese (Pinyin)	Vietnamese Name	Filipino Name	Claimed By	Presently Occupied By
Paracel Islands	Xisha Qundao	Quan Dao Hoang Sa		China Vietnam	Beijing
Pratas Island	Dongsha Qundao			China	Taipei
Spratly Islands	Nansha Qundao	Quan Dao Truong Sa	Kalayaan	China Malaysia Philippines Vietnam	
Amboyna	Anbo Shazhou	Dao An Bang	Kalantiyaw	China Malaysia Philippines Vietnam	Hanoi
Commodore Reef	Siling Jiao		Rizal Reef	China Malaysia Philippines Vietnam	Manila
Flat Island	Antang Dao		Patag	China Philippines Vietnam	Manila
Itu Aba	Taiping Dao	Dao Thai Binh	Ligaw	China Philippines Vietnam	Taipei
Lankiam Cay	Yangxin Zhou		Panata	China Philippines Vietnam	Manila
Loaita	Nanyue Dao	Dao Loai Ta	Kuta	China Philippines Vietnam	Manila
Namyit	Hangxue Dao	Dao Nam Ai	Bingago	China Philippines Vietname	Hanoi
Nanshan	Mahuan Dao		Lawak	China Philippines Vietnam	Manila
Northeast Cay	Beizi Jiao	Dao Song Tu Dong	Parola	China Philippines Vietnam	Manila
Pearson Reef	Bisheng Dao		Hizon	China Philippines Vietnam	Hanoi
Sand Cay	Bailan Jiao	Dao Son Ca		China Philippines Vietnam	Hanoi
Sin Cowe	Jinghong Cao	Dao Sin Tonh	Rurok	China Philippines Vietnam	Hanoi
Southwest Cay	Nanzi Jiao	Dao Song Tu Tay	Pugad	China Philippines Vietnam	Hanoi

(cont. . .)

Table 3.3   Major Garrisoned Islands in the Spratlys (*cont. . .*)

Malaysian/ Standard Name	Chinese (Pinyin)	Vietnamese Name	Filipino Name	Claimed By	Presently Occupied By
Spratly Island	Nanwei Dao	Dao Truong Sa	Lagos	China Vietnam	Hanoi
Swallow Reef	Danwan Jiao			China Malaysia Philippines Vietnam	Kuala Lumpur
Thitu	Zhongye Dao	Dao Thi Tu	Pagasa	China Philippines Vietnam	Manila
West York	Xiyue Dao	Dao Ben Lac	Likas	China Philippines Vietnam	Manila

Adapted from Shepharp, "Maritime Tensions in the South China Sea and the Neighborhood: Some Solutions," 209–211.

brought it into the international limelight.[61] In February 1995, tensions heightened when China increased its military presence in Mischief Reef. This was only 90 miles away from Pagasa Island where the Philippines had its largest military station outside the mainland.[62] China built four structures on Mischief Reef and described them as fishing shelters. A base in Mischief Reef obviously would provide military protection to both mineral and fishing resources.[63] China was accused of breaking both international law and the 1992 Manila Declaration, in which both the parties agreed to solve conflicts through cooperative and peaceful means. The Philippine navy consisted of only a dozen patrol boats and in no way could match their Chinese counterparts. China regarded this occupation as part of its claim to the entire Spratly area based on usage and discovery.

The conflict gathered momentum when the Philippine Department of Energy approved an application made by the U.S. oil company, Vaalco, and its Philippine subsidiary, Alcorn, to conduct an oil exploration exercise near Reed Bank, 400 nms west of Palawan.[64] China immediately protested the move as an infringement of Chinese sovereignty. This situation worsened when the Philippines detained 55 Chinese fishermen. China replied by arresting 35 Philippine fishermen that Beijing claimed had violated Chinese territorial waters.[65] Two further clashes took place in 1996 and 1997 between China and the Philippines. The first of these was in January 1996 when three alleged Chinese vessels were engaged in a 90-minute gun battle with a Philippine navy gunboat near Campones Island. The second clash occurred in April 1997 when the Philippine navy ordered a Chinese speedboat and two fishing boats to leave Scarborough Shoal. In response to this, the Chinese navy sent three warships to survey two islands, Panat and Kota, which were occupied by the Philippines. In late 1998, Chinese workers expanded two of the four shelters, being aware of their future fuel needs. Beijing even started to build fortlike structures on Mischief Reef.[66] The same year, 23 Chinese fishermen were detained for intrusion into Philippine territorial waters. China retaliated in November 1998 by building on islets claimed by the Philippines.[67] Although China announced that it would resolve the Mischief Reef crisis in accordance with the UNCLOS, China's tone changed in 1998. The construction of Chinese facilities on Jackson Atoll and Half Moon Reef, only 70 nm west of Palawan, further strained China's relationship with the Philippines.[68] This was the first militarized dispute that China had with any party other than Vietnam in the SCS. ASEAN, as an organization, decided to strengthen their military preparedness and initiate possible defense cooperation against China. Beijing's moves in the SCS cast doubt and uncertainty regarding China's sincerity about settling issues through negotiations. China apparently not only had intentions to transform itself into a regional maritime power, but also wanted to protect and promote its sea borne trade and fishing industry. China even wanted to create a sea-air-coast island integrated defense system, and it is possible that perhaps what China was looking for was a "transitional stop-gap to its blue water strategy."[69]

MALAYSIA AND CHINA

Even after the Mischief Reef incident, Malaysia felt that China might not use force against them in order to occupy Southern Spratly. However, things changed after the Malaysian navy fired a Chinese vessel wounding four crewmen on March 23, 1995.[70] Following this incident, another clash took place between Manila and Malaysia over the construction of a building on the Investigator Shoal lying 250 km from the nearest recognized territory of either country. Malaysia started building a military facility in response to China's construction of bunkers in Mischief Reef. China criticized Malaysia's action as an encroachment on Chinese territory.[71] Although the dispute did not lead to any further such incidents, it was the first military clash between Malaysia and China.

INDONESIA AND CHINA

China has had no direct conflict with Indonesia; however, the possibility still remains with regard to the Natuna Islands where Indonesia has developed its gas and tourism industry. Indonesia has constructed an airbase on Natuna Besar to conduct its regular air surveillance of the SCS.[72] Although both countries have decided to avoid discussing their bilateral issues at the

national and at the international level, their relationships worsened in July
1994. China began to distribute a map claiming all the Spratly Islands, as
well as the Natuna gas deposits, which were developed by Exxon for Indonesia. Indonesia strongly protested this shift in China's claims.[73] Indonesia and
Vietnam meanwhile were in dispute over the potentially oil-rich continental
shelves surrounding the Indonesian-owned Natuna Islands.

China has realized that its security is very much dependent on maintaining a stable relationship with her neighbors in the Asia-Pacific region.[74] The
1996 multilateral treaty signed by the Shanghai Five was meant to bolster
confidence in favor of China and negate the China threat theory. Originally,
the Shanghai Five group was created on April 26, 1996, with the signing of
the Treaty on Deepening Military Trust in Border Regions in Shanghai by the
heads of states of Kazakhstan, China, Kyrgyzstan, Russia, and Tajikistan.[75]
The establishment of the Shanghai Five was considered as a major step in
consolidating the security and stability of the central Asian region as well as
the entire Asian-Pacific region. However, critics feel that problems concerning the SCS arise due to a disparity between Beijing's promises.[76] Beijing's
desire to seek cooperation, on the one hand, and insisting upon absolute sovereignty, on the other, creates fundamental confusion. China is increasingly
asserting itself in the SCS region, as it has clearly demonstrated by launching
its first aircraft carrier in August 2011. Although, China has stated that it
favors equitable international order and peace, to what extent such considerations will shape China's current defense policy remains to be seen. As Hugh
White comments:

> China seems to be prepared to run the risk so it can exploit these incidents to
> assert its claims. This is what strategic competition between great powers looks
> like. This is how wars start. Welcome to the Asia-Pacific century.[77]

INCIDENTS FROM 2001–2016

Of late, maritime disputes in this region have again become front-page news.
Dubbed by some authors as "a new Persian Gulf," or by some as "a hydrocar-
bons El Dorado," the SCS seems to be shaping up as a strategically volatile
flashpoint capable of generating recurring tensions with intense geopolitical
implications.[78] Vietnam and China are at odds over a Vietnamese survey ship
and Chinese patrol boats in waters off the southern coast of Vietnam. The
Philippines is protesting China's recent unloading of building materials on
Amy Douglas Bank, an area claimed by the Philippines. China's opposition
to a U.S. carrier entering the Yellow Sea for military exercise, its low and
slow relationship with Japan over the Diaoyu Islands, its own naval exercise,

and its overall declaration of the SCS as core interest have led many to conclude that China is increasingly becoming "arrogant and tough."[79]

On March 23, 2001, the hydrographic survey ship, USNS *Bowditch*, was
conducting routine military survey operations in the Chinese-claimed EEZ
in the Yellow Sea. Suddenly a Chinese Jianheu III–class frigate confronted
the ship and ordered it to leave. The *Bowditch* immediately left the area.
However, after a few days, the U.S. embassy filed a diplomatic protest with
the Chinese Ministry of Foreign Affairs. On April 2001, a week after the
Bowditch incident, two Chinese F-8 fighter aircraft intercepted a U.S. EP-3
that was conducting a routine reconnaissance flight about 70 miles south/
southeast of Hainan Island. After making several close approaches to the
American aircraft, one of the F-8s lost control and collided with the EP-3. Not
only is the cause of the collision disputable, but also each party still blames
the other.[80] Some suggest that the United States should attempt to reach a
mutually acceptable solution within the context of the Military Maritime
Consultative Agreement (MMCA), while others call for a negotiation like the
INCSEA (incident at sea) with China to avoid future confrontations of this
nature. In order to avoid such skirmishes and potential miscalculations at sea,
both the U.S. and Chinese forces should vow to respect each other's rights.
Only then the two countries will be able to avoid chances of further miscalculations like this *EP-3* incident. However, such skirmishes continued in the
SCS and things became worse when in 2009 various incidents happened in
the SCS that had significant implications for regional security.

Such developments became self-reinforcing, thereby raising the fundamental question for Southeast Asia's regional security, and they have also
occurred in the context of deteriorating U.S.–Chinese relations and the desire
for a strong U.S. presence in the region.[81] The first incident was the March 8
clash between Chinese vessels and a U.S. ocean surveillance ship off Hainan
followed by the *USNS Victorious*.[82] The United States dispatched the *USNS
Impeccable*, operating 75 miles south of Hainan, to conduct military scientific research related to Chinese submarine activity operating from the Sanya
Naval Base. A PLAN intelligence collection ship declared this operation to
be illegal and urged them to leave. On the following day, five Chinese ships
shadowed the *Impeccable*, including a Bureau of Maritime Fisheries Patrol
Vessel, a State Oceanographic Administration patrol vessel, a Chinese Navy
ocean surveillance ship, and two small Chinese-flagged trawlers. The trawlers
closed in on the *Impeccable*, coming within 15 meters waving Chinese flags
and ordered the *Impeccable* to leave the area. One trawler moved closer to
the *Impeccable* and sprayed it with water from its fire hose. The *Impeccable*
then radioed the Chinese vessels and requested safe passage out of the area.
Two Chinese trawlers next attempted to obstruct the *Impeccable* by stopping
abruptly in front of it and forcing the *Impeccable* to execute an emergency

full stop to avoid a collision. As the *Impeccable* attempted to depart, the crew of one of the Chinese trawlers used a grappling hook to try to snag the sonar array that the *Impeccable* was towing.[83] The confrontation between the *USNS Impeccable* and PLAN vessels was soon followed by the collision of a PLAN submarine with the *USS John S. McCain*, which was one of the three U.S. warships participating in an exercise with six Southeast Asian navies. These incidents sparked additional concern among the ASEAN countries regarding the Sino–U.S. relationship and its potential to affect regional stability.[84]

Another incident took place in the Yellow Sea when the *USNS Victorious*, an ocean surveillance ship, turned its fire hoses on two Chinese fishing vessels. China claimed that the U.S. ship was operating in China's EEZ without permission and had violated both Chinese and international law. This ship was conducting routine operations in the waters between China and the Korean peninsula. The Pentagon, however, accused the Chinese fishing vessels of harassing another U.S. surveillance ship in the SCS near Hainan Island and cited the incident as an example of unsafe Chinese seamanship.[85] The United States thinks that China is playing a dangerous game with a policy of both engagement and limited containment. In response to China's maritime exercise of its A2/AD capabilities in 2010, as well as its general naval buildup, the United States made new arrangements with Australia. The United States also strengthened its position on Guam. Although China follows a kind of hesitant power projection, its A2/AD vector is trying to disengage the exclusive sphere of U.S. influence in the region. In doing so, China is following a *two-vector naval strategy.*[86]

The approval of the 2009 Philippines Baseline Bill by the Philippine Congress and President Arroyo marked another sovereignty dispute over islands and reefs in the SCS. China sternly protested the Philippine bill because it claims Huangyan Island (Scarborough Shoal) and some islands of the Nansha group (the Spratly Islands) as part of Philippine territory. These features are claimed by both China and Vietnam, and Vietnam also protested the bill, warning that the Philippine action threatened peace and stability in the region.[87] Another incident that irritated China was the joint submission by Malaysia and Vietnam in May 2009 to the Commission on the Limits of the Continental Shelf (CLCS).[88] The joint submission of Malaysia and Vietnam suggests that the sovereign rights to the resources to the SCS should be determined by principles governing the continental shelf as measured from the mainland coast. In fact, they took a position whereby no islands in the SCS should be entitled to more than a 12 nms territorial sea. The submission obviously has further implications as to how the hydrocarbon resources of the SCS should be allocated.[89] The Philippines had filed a case and submitted a 4,000-page legal document before the Permanent Court of Arbitration in 2013 against China's massive move in the SCS region. The tribunal was expected to hand down a ruling against this complaint by mid-2016. In fact, the International Court made a landmark decision in early July 2016 in favor of the Philippines. The court has claimed that China's expansive right to sovereignty over the SCS has no legal basis and that China has already harmed the marine environment by their creeping moves in the region. This decision has obviously infuriated the dragon and is a clear case of *negative reward power* for what they have done. However this decision is very significant for other members because it will give them leverage in managing their own maritime disputes with Beijing in the future. In fact this decision has served as a *positive reward power* for them. This ruling has certainly undermined China's long-standing territorial claims in the region and there is a possibility of a *turf war* soon in the region. It's just a matter of time for the international community to see what action China is going to take against the ruling of the Tribunal. Given the situation it is very important for all the claimants to remain calm and restrain themselves from taking any immature steps that might disrupt peace and harmony in the region.

Recently, an 81-year-old former fishing vessel captain, Su Chengfen, claimed that he was able to do fishing all his life in the reef-filled SCS with the help of a handwritten book, which is more than 600 years old. This book depicts routes to various remote islands from Hainan province. This news has created some noise among the SCS claimants. In fact a retired Chinese professor even commented that the book depicts the exact route to Huang-yan Island and it clearly proves that generations of Chinese fishermen have worked on the island.[90] China has also started taking tourists to the disputed Paracel Islands in the SCS for the past three years in a row. Thousands of people exclusively from the Chinese mainland have taken the trip and many even consider it as a patriotic duty. The five-day-long voyage costs between $400–$2000 and takes place in a few reefs and largely uninhabited rocks in the region. The only three islands, which are open for the tourists, are the Quanfu, Yinyu and the Yagong islands.[91] The question remains as to why China is taking such moves and how Beijing is going to justify such initiatives. At the end one has to remember that such moves will only instigate tremendous amount of suspicion, miscalculation, and, finally, escalation of conflicts in the region.

China is also moving fast with its land reclamation strategies in various islands in the SCS region. One plausible interpretation is that China is trying to dominate the entire area militarily by establishing a chain of outposts in the SCS region. China's land reclamation strategy is still on. In fact, Beijing has started building an artificial island by pumping sand at the Johnson South reef since 2015.

This has led to serious questions on its intention. Even high-resolution satellite images show that Woody Island, occupied by China since 1956, is also undergoing a major expansion of its runway and airport facilities. Additional land reclamation is also under way on the Woody Island. Besides, 80 km southwest of Woody, on Duncan Island (seized by China from Vietnam in 1974), satellite images show landfill has increased the size of the island by approximately 50 percent since April 2014. The island also houses a military garrison, four radar domes, a concrete manufacturing plant, and a port that has recently been expanded via dredging and coral cutting.

The SCS dispute can be described as a great bargaining game in which the littoral countries consider their ownership of this potentially rich maritime zone in zero-sum terms.[92] Those with the most bargaining power leave the game with the biggest reward as opposed to those who have no bargaining power. China, being the most powerful player in this dispute, exercises a relatively aggressive policy toward other claimants by maintaining a very staunch position. A particularly serious issue associated with this zero-sum game is the lack of agreement on some fundamental legal principles relating to boundary delimitation, maritime jurisdiction, and the 1982 UNCLOS. On the one hand, China authorizes the use of force to preserve its core interest in this region and, on the other hand, tries to woo its neighbors' faith through its charm diplomacy. China is continuously upgrading its military technologies and maintaining a strong physical presence in this region. As You Ji observes, "the PLAN's presence in the Spratlys is more political than military for the time being."[93] It is thus hard to determine whether China is actually trying to establish a maritime sphere of influence and hegemony in the SCS. As Sun Tzu once commented: "Never let out your real intentions. Lull your adversaries by all possible means. Hide your capabilities."[94]

The following chapter will discuss the involvement of China with other Asian claimants, its Arctic strategy, and the involvement of major powers like the United States, and India in the SCS conflict.

NOTES

1. John Bradford, "The Growing Prospects for Maritime Security Cooperation in Southeast Asia," *Naval War College Review* 58, no. 3 (2005).
2. Michael Richardson, "Commentary on Energy and Geopolitics in the South China Sea by Michael Richardson," http://www.iseas.edu.sg/aseanstudiescentre/ascdf2c1.pdf, 4.
3. Geoffrey Till, "The South China Sea Dispute: An International History," in *Security and International Politics in the South China Sea: Towards a Co-operative Management Regime*, ed. Sam Bateman and Ralf Emmers (London: Routledge, 2009), 38.

4. Ian Townsend-Gault, "Legal And Political Perspectives On Sovereignty Over The Spratly Islands" (paper presented at the Workshop on the South China Sea Conflict Organized by the Center for Development and Environment, University of Oslo, Oslo, April 24–26, 1999).

5. Richardson, "Commentary on Energy and Geopolitics in the South China Sea by Michael Richardson," 5.

6. MakJoon Num, "Sovereignty in ASEAN and the Problem of Maritime Cooperation in the South China Sea," in *Security and International Politics in the South China Sea: Towards a Co-operative Management Regime*, ed. Sam Bateman and Ralf Emmers (London: Routledge, 2009), 121.

7. Liselotte Odgaard, "Deterrence and Cooperation in the South China Sea," *Contemporary Southeast Asia* 23, no. 2 (August 2001).

8. Tony Tan, "Policing the Sea Is a Job for Everyone," *Straits Times*, June 3, 2003.

9. Bradford, "The Growing Prospects For Maritime Security Cooperation in Southeast Asia."

10. Stein Tonnesson, "The History of the Dispute," in *War or Peace in the South China Sea?* ed. Timo Kivimaki (Copenhagen: NIAS Press, 2002), 6.

11. Ibid., 6–7.

12. Ibid., 8.

13. Ibid., 8–9.

14. Ibid.

15. Chin Yoon Chin, "Potential For Conflict in the Spratly Islands," Master's Thesis (Naval Postgraduate School, Monterey, CA, 2003), 10.

16. Tonnesson, "The History of the Dispute," 8–9.

17. Ibid., 9.

18. Ibid.

19. Ibid., 11.

20. Ibid., 6.

21. Ibid., 11.

22. Ibid., 12.

23. Omar Saleem, "The Spratly Islands Dispute: China Defines the New Millennium," *American University Law Review* 15, no. 3 (2000): 527.

24. Eric Hyer, "The South China Sea Dispute: Implications of China's Earlier Territorial Settlements," *Pacific Affairs* 68, no. 1 (Spring 1995): 37.

25. Ibid., 52.

26. Chin, "Potential For Conflict in the Spratly Islands," 17.

27. John Garver, "China's Push Through the South China Sea: The Interactions of Bureaucratic and National Interests," *The China Quarterly* 132 (December 1992): 1007.

28. Ibid.,1007–8.

29. Ibid., 1017.

30. Nayan Chanda, "South China Sea: Treacherous Shoals," *Far Eastern Economic Review* (August 13, 1992): 14–17.

31. Leszek Buszynski and Iskandar Sazlan, "Maritime Claims and Energy Cooperation in the South China Sea," *Contemporary Southeast Asia* 29, no. 1 (2007).

32. Sulan Chen, *Instrumental and Induced Cooperation: Environmental Politics in the South China Sea* (College Park, MD: University of Maryland, 2005).

33. The Fiery Cross reef has a linear shape aligned south-west to north-east. Its long axis measures 14 nautical miles while the maximum width is 4 nautical miles with a total area of 110 square kilometers. At high tide the whole reef gets submerged except for a prominent rock, which is one meter high. The reef has an airstrip and a marine observation station built in 1988. Additionally, China built a navy harbor. This reef is incapable of supporting any human habitation since it lacks fresh water and fertile soil.

34. Garver, "China's Push Through the South China Sea," 1009.

35. Daniel Dzurek. "The Spratly Islands Dispute: Who's On First?" *International Boundaries Research Unit Maritime Briefing* 2, no. 1 (1996).

36. Marius Gjetnes, "The Legal Regime of Islands in The South China Sea." Master's Thesis (University of Oslo, Norway, 2000), 77–8.

37. Mark Valencia, "The Spratly Islands: Dangerous Ground in the South China Sea," *The Pacific Review* 1, no. 4 (1988): 439.

38. Ibid., 438.

39. Dzurek, "The Spratly Islands Dispute: Who's On First?"

40. Chang Pao, "A New Scramble for the South China Sea Islands," *Contemporary Southeast Asia* 12, no. 1 (June 1990): 25.

41. The Non-Aligned Movement (NAM) was started by Indian Prime minister Jawaharlal Nehru, Yugoslavian President Marshal Tito, and Egyptian President Nasser. The first meeting was held in Bandung, Indonesia, in 1955.

42. Chanda, "South China Sea: Treacherous Shoals," 15.

43. Dzurek, "The Spratly Islands Dispute: Who's On First?"

44. Marko Milivojevic, "The Spratly and Paracel Islands Conflict," *Survival* 31, no. 1 (January–February 1989): 74.

45. Dzurek, "The Spratly Islands Dispute: Who's On First?"

46. Although, the Sino-French Treaty of 1887 roughly demarcated the Sino-Vietnamese border, no accurate demarcation ever took place. This war began with numerous armed skirmishes along the border and became a source of tension since then.

47. Tridib Chakraborti, "The Territorial Claims in South China Sea: Probing Persistent Uncertainties," in *Peoples Republic of China at Fifty: Politics, Economy and Foreign Relations*, ed. Arun Kumar Banerji and Purusottam Bhattacharya (New Delhi: Lancer Publication), 186.

48. Kim Shee, "The South China Sea in China's Strategic Thinking," *Contemporary Southeast Asia* 19, no. 4 (March 1998): 377.

49. Niklas Swanstrom, "Conflict Management and Negotiations in the South China Sea: The ASEAN Way?" Online publication of the Virtual Library of South China Sea (1999): 98, http://community.middlebury.edu/~scs/docs/Swanstrom.pdf.

50. Valencia, "The Spratly Islands: Dangerous Ground in the South China Sea," 78.

51. Michael Klare, *Resource Wars: The New Landscape of Global Conflict* (New York: Henry Holt and Company, LLC, 2001).

52. Valencia, "The Spratly Islands: Dangerous Ground in the South China Sea," 79.

53. Chakraborti, "The Territorial Claims in South China Sea," 196.

54. Tai Ming Cheung. "The Balance Tilts," *Far Eastern Economic Review* (September 29, 1988): 40–1.

55. Donald Weatherbee, "The South China Sea: From Zone of Conflict to Zone of Peace?" in *East Asian Conflict Zones: Prospects for Regional Stability and De-escalation*, ed. Lawrence Grinter and Kihl Young (London: Macmillan Press, 1987), 130.

56. Chakraborti, "The Territorial Claims in South China Sea," 186.

57. Ibid., 187.

58. Ibid.

59. Ibid.

60. Allen Shepharp, "Maritime Tensions in the South China Sea and the Neighborhood: Some Solutions," *Studies in Conflict and Terrorism* 21, no. 2 (April–June 1994): 209–11.

61. Mark Valencia, "Mischief at the Reef," *Far Eastern Economic Review* (May 20, 1999), 31.

62. Ibid.

63. Chakraborti, "The Territorial Claims in South China Sea," 195.

64. Ibid., 191.

65. Swanstrom, "Conflict Management and Negotiations in the South China Sea: The ASEAN Way?" 98.

66. Valencia, "Mischief at the Reef," 31.

67. Ibid.

68. Mark Valencia, Jon M. Van Dyke, and Noel A. Ludwig, *Sharing the Resources of the South China Sea* (Leiden, The Netherlands: Martinus Nijhoff Publishers, 1997), 81.

69. Shee, "The South China Sea in China's Strategic Thinking," 382.

70. Swanstrom,, "Conflict Management and Negotiations in the South China Sea: The ASEAN Way?" 99.

71. Chakraborti, "The Territorial Claims in South China Sea,"197.

72. Ibid., 193.

73. Valencia, Van Dyke, and Ludwig, *Sharing the Resources of the South China Sea*, 27.

74. For example, in November 2004, China and the ASEAN agreed to gradually remove tariffs and create the world's largest free trade area by 2010. Another example is the Treaty of Good-Neighborliness and Friendly Cooperation signed by Russia and China.

75. On June 15, 2001, Uzbekistan became a new member and signed the Declaration of Shanghai Cooperation Organization. And it was renamed as the Shanghai Cooperation Organization.

76. Rita Akpan, "China, the Spratly Islands Territorial Dispute and Multilateral Cooperation– An Exercise in Realist Rhetoric or Mere Diplomatic Posturing?

A Critical Review," CEPMLP Gateway (February 2003): 4, http://www.dundee.ac.uk/cepmlp/gateway/index.php?news=27994.

77. Peter Hartcher, "US finds unwilling partner in China to avert potential crisis in region," Sydney Morning Herald, August 17, 2011, http://www.smh.com.au/world/us-finds-unwilling-partner-in-china-to-avert-potential-crisis-in-region-20110816-1iwge.html.

78. Pan Chengxin, "Is the South China Sea a new 'Dangerous Ground' for US-China rivalry?" *East Asia Forum* (May 2011), http://www.eastasiaforum.org/2011/05/24/is-the-south-china-sea-a-new-dangerous-ground-for-us-china-rivalry/.

79. Da Wei, "Has China Become 'Tough'?" *China Security* 6, no. 3 (2010): 35–42.

80. Raul Pedrozo, "Close Encounters at Sea: The USNS Impeccable Incident," *Naval War College Review* 62, no.3 (Summer 2009): 101–11.

81. Mark J. Valencia, "The South China Sea: Back to the Future?" *Global Asia: A Journal of the East Asia Foundation* (December 2010), http://www.globalasia.org/V5N4_Winter_2010/Mark_J_Valencia.html.

82. Mark J. Valencia, "Tempting the Dragon," March 12, 2009, http://nautilus.org/napsnet/napsnet-policy-forum/tempting-the-dragon/#sect1.

83. Carlyle Thayer, "Recent Developments in the South China Sea: Implications for Peace, Stability and Cooperation in the Region," in *The South China Sea: Cooperation For Regional Security and Development: Proceedings of the International Workshop co-organized by the Diplomatic Academy of Vietnam and the Vietnam Lawyers' Association*, ed. Thuy, Tran Truong, 125–38 (Hanoi: Diplomatic Academy of Vietnam, November 2009), http://nghiencuubiendong.vn/en/datbase-on-south-china-sea-study/doc_details/36-the-south-china-sea-cooperation-for-regional-security-and-development.

84. Ibid.

85. Jane Macartney, "Chinese and American ships clash again in Yellow Sea," *Sunday Times*, May 6, 2009, http://www.infowars.com/chinese-and-american-ships-clash-again/.

86. Marvin Taylor," PRC Area-Denial Capabilities and American Power Projection," Prospect's Blog, June 2012, http://prospectjournalblog.wordpress.com/.

87. Michael Richardson, "Commentary on Energy and Geopolitics in the South China Sea by Michael Richardson," http://www.iseas.edu.sg/aseanstudiescentre/ascdf2c1.pdf.

88. Sam Bateman, "The Regime of the South China Sea—The Significance of the Declaration on the Conduct of Parties," https://blog.canpan.info/oprf/img/858/dr.bateman_presentation.pdf.

89. Robert Beckman, "South China Sea: Worsening Dispute or Growing Clarity in Claims," RSIS Commentaries, August 16, 2010, http://www.rsis.edu.sg/publications/Perspective/RSIS0902010.pdf.

90. John Sudworth, "South China Sea: The Mystery of Missing Books and Maritime Claims," BBC News, June 19, 2016.

91. "South China Sea: Chinese Tours of Disputed Waters," BBC News, June 21, 2016. http://www.bbc.com/news/world-asia-china-36562117

92. Num, "Sovereignty in ASEAN and the Problem of Maritime Cooperation in the South China Sea," 121.

93. James Manicom, "IR Theory and Asia's Maritime Territorial Disputes" (paper presented to the Australasian Political Studies Association Conference, University of Newcastle, September 2006).

94. Maj. Gen. (rtd) Vinod Saighal, "International Workshop on 'South China Sea: Cooperation for Security and Development'," in *The South China Sea: Cooperation For Regional Security and Development: Proceedings of the International Workshop co-organized by the Diplomatic Academy of Vietnam and the Vietnam Lawyers' Association*, ed. Thuy, Tran Truong, 290–304 (Hanoi: Diplomatic Academy of Vietnam, November 2009), http://nghiencuubiendong.vn/en/datbase-on-south-china-sea-study/doc_details/36-the-south-china-sea-cooperation-for-regional-security-and-development, p. 12.

Chapter 4

Struggle for Power in the South China Sea

Ultimate excellence lies . . . not in winning every battle, but in defeating the enemy, without ever fighting.

—Sun Tzu

The SCS is regarded as a highly volatile environment because of the potential energy resources beneath the sea and an apparent willingness on the part of claimant states to use military force to defend access to these resources.[1] As the Dutch legal scholar Hugo Grotius argued in the *Mare Liberum* (*Freedom of the Seas*, published in 1609), the ocean's bounty is inexhaustible, as limitless as the air; thus, it "cannot become a possession of any one." In fact, the SCS and the coastal passage from Malaysia to Russia have become an area of crucial economic interest to all. Territorial disputes in the South and East China Seas, along with military buildups by Beijing and Tokyo, evidence a highly unstable relationship.[2] This argument is strengthened further by assessments that point to a growing "energy nationalism" across Asia.[3]

In many ways, the SCS dispute is typical of the post-Cold War security situation in East Asia. With the decreasing significance of U.S.–Soviet and Sino-Soviet competition, territorial disputes, which received little attention during the Cold War, have reemerged. Although China and the United States are not engaged in a maritime boundary dispute, fundamental disagreements exist between them over the laws that govern the conduct of vessels at sea. Such disagreements over navigational freedom, not least of military vessels, in coastal state waters have already triggered a number of incidents between the two. This chapter discusses China's relationship with other Asian states claiming rights to the SCS, and analyzes the involvement of major powers like the United States and India. The chapter ends with a brief discussion of Beijing's reconsideration of the SCS dispute in light of its Arctic Strategy.

THE WATERGATE IMBROGLIO

China vs. Asian Claimants

Tensions are indeed rising almost every day in the SCS region. Rivalries, which once revolved around issues like sovereignty, fisheries, energy resources, and maritime navigational rights, are now being overshadowed by major power initiatives to gain greater strategic influence in the region. The People's Liberation Army (PLA), with some 1.25 million ground troops (the largest in the world) is on target to build a modern and regionally focused force by 2020. While celebrating its 85th anniversary, the PLA made it clear that China's maritime interests are nonnegotiable. Regarding the SCS, China's Ministry of Defense spokesperson, Geng Yanshen, declared that China not only has indisputable sovereignty over the SCS but also has sufficient historical and legal backing to underpin its claims. At the same time, the military has denied that they are preparing for war in the SCS. Such actions by China, amid its rising nationalism as well as extended military exercises in the area, have provided a diplomatic opportunity for the United States and even pushed some ASEAN countries into the U.S. corner.[4]

In June 2008, Vietnam's Prime Minister Nguyen Tan Dung made a trip to the United States and met President Bush. In a joint statement released after the Bush–Dung meeting, both sides agreed to hold regular high-level talks on security and strategic issues. For its part, Vietnam followed a "3 nos" policy: no military alliances, no foreign bases, and no reliance on another country to combat a third country. While accelerating the modernization of its navy, Vietnam encouraged the United States and ASEAN to internationalize the problem and hold regular dialogue with China to manage tensions.[5] China was unhappy about the building up of a deeper U.S.–Vietnam security tie. There are, however, clear differences between China and Vietnam's approaches to initiating policies and to employing conflict resolution techniques when addressing disputes in the South as well as the East China Seas. Beijing is also trying to pressure Hanoi to accept a joint exploration and production agreement pertaining to energy fields located off the coast of Vietnam so that no foreign oil companies are able to enter into energy deals with Vietnam. However, this tactic has proved to be unsuccessful since both BP and ExxonMobil have indicated their intention to proceed with such deals. Vietnam and China also differed on the question of multilateral negotiations. In May 2009, China announced a unilateral three-month moratorium on fishing in the

SCS in order top reserve fish stocks, address illegal fishing, and prevent the arrest of Chinese fishermen and other forms of harassment. This particular season was regarded as the best for Vietnamese fishing. Vietnam immediately lodged a diplomatic protest. In one instance, a Chinese fishery vessel sank a Vietnamese boat, seized three others, and took 37 crew members into custody near the Paracel Islands. The Vietnamese Foreign Ministry issued another protest note to the Chinese Embassy in Hanoi.[6] China's assertiveness appeared to have backfired because the judgment came in Vietnam's favor. Although Beijing's military buildup in the SCS does not necessarily indicate that Beijing will use force to occupy more islands, it does, however, suggest that Beijing is keeping its options open.

In 2011, China and Vietnam held four high-level meetings in which the SCS dispute was discussed. The first was with regard to the China's unilateral fishing ban. On May 11, 2011, the Haikou Municipal Government issued an announcement imposing China's annual unilateral fishing ban in the SCS to protect dwindling fish stocks during the spawning season. Vietnam immediately issued a verbal protest stating, "China's unilateral execution of a fishing ban in the East Sea is a violation of Vietnam's sovereignty over the Hoang Sa [Paracel] archipelago, as well as the country's sovereignty and jurisdiction over its exclusive economic zone and continental shelf."[7] Vietnam also protested the deployment of a Chinese fishery administration vessel, Leizhou 44261, to patrol the waters around the Paracel Islands, which led to the first cable cutting incident. On May 26, 2011, three Chinese maritime surveillance ships accosted the Binh Minh 02, a Vietnamese seismic survey ship operating in Block 148, in an incident that lasted three hours. Maritime surveillance ship No. 84 cut a cable towing seismic monitoring equipment. The next day Vietnam lodged a diplomatic protest with China's ambassador claiming that the actions of the Chinese maritime surveillance ships violated international law and Vietnam's sovereignty. This was followed by the second cable-cutting incident in June of the same year when Chinese fishing boat No. 62226, equipped with a "cable cutting device," snared the cable of the Viking II seismic survey ship operating in the vicinity of Vanguard Bank.[8] This was followed by live-fire exercises after the Chinese ambassador to the Philippines called on Vietnam and the Philippines to cease oil exploration. Vietnam immediately raised the stakes by announcing a live-fire exercise. Vietnam's Northern Maritime Safety Corporation issued a notice that two live-firing exercises would be held on June 13, 2011, near Hon Ong Island. Vietnam's Foreign Ministry characterized such exercises as a routine annual training activity of the Vietnamese navy. The *Global Times* of China, however, commented that the live-firing exercises carried out by Vietnam were the "lowest form of nationalism to create a new enmity between the people of the two countries."[9] It was further commented that, "Hanoi seems to be looking to dissipate domestic pressure and buck up morale at home while at the same time further drawing in the concern of international society over the SCS dispute."[10]

In April 2011, a joint venture was set up between PetroVietnam's Petroleum Technical Services Corporation and CGG Veritas of France to conduct seismic surveys off the Vietnam coast.[11] According to the chairman of the China National Offshore Oil Corporation (CNOOC), "disruptive" activities in the SCS result in an annual loss of about 20 million tons of oil for China, or about 40 percent of its total offshore production. In order to curb such losses, China announced that it would step up maritime patrols by at least 10 percent in light of increasing incursions into its territorial waters. CNOOC further declared its intention to invest US $31 billion to drill 800 deep-water wells in the East Sea, Yellow Sea, and SCS with the aim of producing 500 million tons of oil by 2020. China also announced its plan to construct a mega oil and gas-drilling platform to be used by the CNOOC in the SCS. Such developments were followed by huge demonstrations from a broad section of the Vietnamese student community using Facebook and other social networking sites. The protestors held placards reading, "Down with China," "The Spratlys and Paracels belong to Vietnam," and "Stop Violating Vietnam's Territory."[12] The growing enmity between nationalists in China and Vietnam has even spilled over into cyberspace. More than 200 Vietnamese websites were subject to cyber attacks. Among the sites affected were those of the Ministry of Agriculture and Rural Development and the Ministry of Foreign Affairs where hackers succeeded in posting Chinese flags and slogans.[13]

Beijing's recent offer to Taipei for the joint exploration of resource-rich waters of the SCS at the expense of others has created great unease. There are several considerations here. First, fuels shipped from the Persian Gulf, western Africa, and China drive Taiwan's economy. Hence, if this supply gets cut off, then Taiwan's economic activity would obviously be jeopardized. Second, it is estimated that underneath the SCS lie oil and natural gas reserves that could meet more than 60 years of current demand. Third, Taipei does not have the military power or economic confidence to handle such situations. Its diplomatic isolation, shaky energy situation, far-off location from Itu Aba Island, and the fact that it is not a party to the UNCLOS have all further complicated its predicament. CNOOC and Taiwan's state-owned oil refiner, CPC Corporation, have collaborated before and conducted joint surveys in the Tai-Chao basin. This has infuriated Washington, Manila, and particularly Hanoi. Evidencing Vietnam's dissatisfaction with the China–Taiwan alliance, and particularly with Taiwan, 42 Vietnamese intrusions were counted within 6 km of Taiwan-controlled Taiping Island in 2010, followed by 106 in 2011, and 41 in 2012.[14] The Vietnamese have even fired at the Taiwanese coast guard station on the island. Taiwan has started to view Vietnam as their enemy rather than China and thinks that the PLA would be capable of protecting them. Hence, the concept of cross-strait military cooperation is gaining prominence, but there are certainly a few risks involved for Taipei.

China's two-track hard/soft policy toward SCS disputes indicates a pattern it has been following in both settled cases and those that are unsettled, such as the dispute (East China sea) with Japan over islets known as Senkaku in Japan and Diaoyu in China. The Japanese government declared that it would buy the privately owned islets, which upset China. In response, China decided to send two patrol ships to safeguard the islets. China is strongly opposed to any application of the 1960 U.S.–Japan Treaty of Mutual Cooperation and Security in its dispute over Senkaku/Diaoyu. While Japan has decided to pursue a "mutually beneficial strategic partnership" with China, which would allow both economic engagement and develop better relations,[15] it is still building up its self-defense forces (SDFs) in reaction to China's expanding maritime capabilities. As such, it has been strengthening the ability of its SDFs to operate at long range. With the passage of the Law Relating to Measures for Preserving the Peace and Security of Japan, the permitted area of its SDF activity has been expanded to encompass "peripheral areas" lying outside of its main islands, including the SCS. The Japanese government even declared that in emergencies Japanese forces would be permitted to conduct missions in areas outside Japan.[16] Japan even plans to build either two medium-sized aircraft carriers or a large transport vessel with displacement in excess of 15,000 tons. Japan is also conducting military exchange visits and joint exercises with countries in Southeast Asia and South Asia as well as strengthening its relations with Russia and other Central Asian nations. The most important aim is to ensure balance in the Asia-Pacific region and also to counterbalance asymmetric dependence. As Hughes points out, this is a quiet military hedging game that Japan is playing with China;[17] as Japan is mostly concerned with China's A2/AD aircraft and maritime power projection capabilities both in the SCS and the East China Sea. As far as the "Near Seas" is concerned, China pursues a policy of maintaining strict sovereignty and jurisdiction along with A2/AD capabilities to deter outside influence.

South Korea and Japan are themselves in a sovereignty dispute over the Liancourt Rocks (known as Takeshima in Japan and Dokdo in South Korea) in the Sea of Japan.[18] China is becoming a threat to South Korea due to its increasing ability to project power into the SLOCs around the Korean Peninsula. Therefore, South Korea is trying to be less economically dependent on China and also developing its own military modernization program. However, the situation became complicated when the South Korean president, Lee Myung-bak, visited the disputed islands of Takeshima.[19] This incident has raised diplomatic tensions since the islands are historically claimed both by Japan and South Korea but have been occupied by South Korea since 1954. The islands are 230,000 square miles in size with no fresh water; however, they have extensive fishing grounds and could also contain huge gas deposits. In response, the Japanese government recalled its own envoy and summoned the South Korean ambassador in Tokyo. Matters are thus getting increasingly more complicated amidst rising tensions, even in the East China Sea region. Southeast Asian countries are seemingly becoming more concerned about Beijing's increasingly assertive behavior in regional waters.[20]

Recently, in tropical waters off the coast of the Philippines, a standoff between Chinese fishing boats, two Chinese law enforcement vessels, and a Philippine Navy ship attracted a lot of international attention. It was reported that the squabble was over some rare corals, clams, and poached sharks that the Philippine Navy were trying to retrieve from the Chinese fishing boats operating in the Scarborough Shoal of the SCS. According to the Philippines Department of Foreign Affairs, China's increased activities in the Spratly Islands have led to six to seven major incursions into waters. In fact, Joker Arroyo commented, "Not even a resolution of concern or of sympathy had been issued by ASEAN. We are left to fend for ourselves. What happened to us? We're like orphans . . . without allies. That's our dilemma."[21] While the Philippines have preferred to negotiate bilaterally with China, Cambodia, and Laos are getting pro-China on this issue.[22]

The Philippine government's move to rename a portion of the SCS will not affect China's similar claim to sovereignty over areas within the sea. Philippine President Aquino signed an administrative order to formally name a maritime area in the western part of the country as the "West Philippine Sea."[23] The recent announcements of joint oil and gas exploration by the Philippines and Vietnam are viewed by Beijing as a challenge. Again in February 2011, Forum Energy, an Anglo-French consortium based in the United Kingdom, concluded a two-year survey of oil and gas resources in the SCS. President Aquino awarded Forum Energy an exploration contract in the Reed Bank area. This has raised some concerns in China.

On February 25, 2011, three Philippines fishing vessels, *F/V Jaime DLS*, *F/V Mama Lydia DLS*, and *F/V Maricris 12*, were operating in the waters off Jackson Atoll, 140 nms west of Palawan. These fishing vessels were approached by a Jianghu-V Class missile frigate, *Dongguan 560*, which asked them to leave. On March 2, 2011, two Chinese white-painted patrol boats, No. 71 and No. 75, ordered *MV Veritas Voyager*, a Forum Energy Plc survey vessel operating in the Reed Bank area off Palawan Island, to leave. The Philippines responded by dispatching two OV-10 aircraft to investigate. The Chinese boats departed immediately. The third incident took place on May 6, 2011, when a Chinese marine vessel with a flat bed was sighted in

Bombay Shoal. Soon after this incident, on May 19, 2011, the Armed Forces of the Philippines (AFP) claimed that two Chinese jet fighters allegedly flew into the Philippines' airspace near Palawan. This initial report was not confirmed and appeared to be the least substantiated among other reported incidents of Chinese incursions. Again, on May 21, 2011, Chinese Marine Surveillance ship No. 75 and Salvage/Research Ship No. 707 were observed heading toward Southern Bank. Then on May 24, 2011, Filipino fishermen reported seeing a Chinese maritime surveillance vessel and PLAN ships unloading steel posts, building materials, and a buoy near Likas and Patag in the Iroquois Reef–Amy Douglas Bank, 100 nms off Palawan.[24]

Meanwhile, President Aquino met with President Bambang Susilo Yudhoyono and expressed his full support for Indonesia's leadership role as ASEAN Chair. President Yudhoyono expressed his hope that the SCS could become a "zone of possible economic cooperation."[25] The Philippines also announced a new U.S. training program for its naval forces to enable them to better carry out their mission of providing security for oil exploration activities in the SCS. While launching the new Zone of Peace, Freedom, Friendship and Cooperation (ZOPFF/C) initiative, President Aquino explained, "What is ours is ours, and with what is disputed, we can work towards joint cooperation."[26] The United States and the Philippines further announced plans to expand intelligence sharing and cooperation on maritime security amidst growing tension in the SCS.

Philippine President Aquino's plan to begin drilling off Reed Bank, and how China will react to this incident is an open question. Manila's announcement to open new blocks off Palawan for hydrocarbon exploration has already triggered conflict between the two countries. China objected by arguing that some of the blocks are in areas over which China has rights and jurisdiction. Although the Philippines' position is based on the distinction in UNCLOS between "islands and rocks,"[27] this situation is complicated because China argues that some of the features near Reed Bank, such as Nansha Island, are "islands" under UNCLOS since they are naturally formed areas of land above water at high tide.

Chinese civilian maritime enforcement ships confronted a Philippines' navy frigate in a standoff over the Scarborough Shoal, a triangular-shaped chain of reefs and rocks enclosing an area of 150 skm located between the Macclesfield Bank and the Luzon Island of the Philippines in the SCS. Both China and the Philippines claim that Scarborough Shoal is an integral part of their national territory. China refers to Scarborough Shoal as Huangyan Island and asserts indisputable sovereignty over the island and adjacent waters on the basis of historical discovery. The Philippines refer to Scarborough Shoal as Panatag Shoal, which falls within its 200 nms EEZ. One recent clash began when a Philippine reconnaissance aircraft spotted five Chinese fishing vessels in the lagoon. The Philippine Navy investigated the Chinese vessels and discovered giant clams, coral, and sharks, species protected under Philippine law and the Convention on International Trade in Endangered species of Wild Flora and Fauna.[28] China and the Philippines formally protested each other's actions. In an effort to lower tensions, the Philippines withdrew the navy frigate, replacing it with a Coast Guard cutter. The dispute still simmers. While China says it wants to negotiate bilaterally, the Philippines has adopted a three-pronged strategy—legal, political, and diplomatic—and took its case to the International Tribunal on Law of the Sea. China increased pressure by issuing a travel advisory that led to cancellation of 80 scheduled Chinese tour groups and charter flights to the Philippines, temporarily halted imports of Filipino bananas on a pretext of infestation, and imposed an unilateral fishing ban in the area. The Philippines issued its own fishing ban in the shoal.[29] China has no immediate plans to pull out its vessels from Scarborough Shoal. Rather, China is sending vessel *"Nanhaijiu 115"*[30] in order to assist Chinese fishing boats affected by inclement weather and strong tides.

The Philippines and the United States have conducted annual Balikatan military exercises, and China announced that it intends to produce its first deep-water mega oil-drilling rig.[31] China also plans to deploy unmanned aerial vehicles (UAVs) and to construct 11 UAV bases along its coastline in order to conduct remote-sensing marine surveillance.[32] Roberto Romulo, a former foreign secretary of the Philippines, stated that China is not only testing the United States but also eating the United States's lunch in Southeast Asia.[33] The deputy chief of the PLA, Gen. Ma Xiaotian, insisted that the South China issue is not the United States's business but it is rather an issue between China and its neighbors. China is also planning to set up a communication network to link the islets in the SCS. This will include 51 base stations on islets, 104 base stations on boats, and eight undersea cables, as well as cover islets in the SCS, including the islets of the Paracel Islands, Macclesfield Bank, and Spratly Islands. This is a part of China's bid to "tighten its grip" on these island groups, which were designated by China as Sansha City of the Hainan province.[34] The biggest drawback is that Sansha sits in the SCS, where rival territorial claims have intensified overtime. China has not only deployed its first aircraft carrier, but it has also projected its power in the area by sabotaging Vietnam's oil exploration efforts in recent years.

The China-based *Global Times* commented: "If these countries don't want to change their ways with China, they will need to prepare for the sounds of cannons. We need to be ready for that, as it may be the only way for the disputes in the sea to be resolved."[35] Each side is asking the other to take concrete measures to reduce the conflict, while increasing their own presence. China sent ships to Huayang Reef on July 1, 2012, and anchored them to the northeast of Yongshu Reef after covering a distance of 1,800 nms. China reports that it is considering setting up a military body in its newly established city of Sansha that administers Chinese territory in the West Philippine Sea. This action has angered both Vietnam and the Philippines, and they have declared that it is a violation of international law. Around 1,000 people inhabit the city on the island of Yongxing, also known as Woody Island. China announced that the island city would host troops and serve as the administrative center for islands claimed by Vietnam, the Philippines, and other neighboring nations. Beijing is determined to block any unified effort from rival claimants. Such a hardline approach was also visible at the annual foreign ministers meeting of ASEAN in 2012. China is spending nearly $1 billion on a locally built 981 ultra-deep water Haiyang Shiyou offshore oil rig owned by CNOOC, which will explore disputed areas of the SCS and also drill south of Hong Kong in an area within Beijing's realm.[36] Eventually, CNOOC has plans to explore more oil-rich waters where Vietnam, the Philippines, Taiwan, Malaysia, and Brunei have overlapping territorial claims.

THE DRAGON VS. THE EAGLE AND THE ELEPHANT

With the exception of India, and possibly Japan, all Asian nations have asymmetrical relationships with China. However, India is increasingly getting involved in the wider Asia-Pacific region as part of its "Look East Policy," which aims to strengthen its influence in Southeast Asia. India hosted the ASEAN–India Commemorative Summit in New Delhi in December 2012 to mark the 20th anniversary of the ASEAN–India dialogue partnership. The theme of the summit was "ASEAN–India Partnership for Peace and Shared Prosperity," and it also marked the 10th anniversary of ASEAN–India summit-level partnership.

In 2002, both the Indian and the U.S. navies worked together to ensure safe transit through the Straits of Malacca. India also signed an agreement with Singapore in 2003 to improve maritime security and counterterrorism activities. Both the Indian and the Indonesian navies performed joint patrols of the Six Degree Channel lying between Aceh and the Nicobar Islands.[37] India seemed to be worried about the rapidly modernizing Chinese military. In fact, General Deepak Kapoor commented, "We need to take note of likely implications of China's military modernization [and] improvement of infrastructure in the Tibet Autonomous Region, which could impact our security in the long-term."[38] China is viewed as a serious peer competitor for India, since, like India, China is also shifting its military focus from a predominantly land-based strategy to a blue water strategy. For example, China is building ports (in Gwadar, Pakistan) and strengthening maritime relations in a number of Indian Ocean region (IOR) locations. Apart from India and Pakistan's historical conflicts, the China–Pakistan connection is inflammatory due to a strategic situation described as India's "Hormuz Dilemma."[39] This refers to India's dependence on imports passing through the Strait of Hormuz in close proximity to Pakistan's Makran coast and emphasizes the danger of a strong China–Pakistan relationship in that area of the IOR. In fact, China's encroachment into the IOR is a matter of grave concern to India. Many even view the PLA's move against India as a part of its strategic encirclement.[40] Although India and China have signed a treaty to maintain peace and tranquility along the disputed border, talks regarding a 3,500-km disputed frontier have hardly made any progress.[41]

Scobell predicts that China and India are likely to witness "simmering tensions" in their relations.[42] From China's perspective, India's actions in Tibet are viewed as affecting China's sovereignty and territorial integrity. Commenting on the 1962 war, Xia Liping stated, "It was not a purely military action, but a complicated political, diplomatic, and military war."[43] Apparently, the main objective of the Chinese government was "not to recover the territory, but to wipe out more Indian effective strength so as to give more serious lessons to the Indian Army."[44] The 2010–2011 annual report by the Indian Defense Ministry stated, "[I] t is watchful of China's increasing military capabilities as well as the implication of China's evolving military profile in the immediate and extended neighborhood."[45] The 2007 Indian Navy document, *Freedom to use the Seas: India's Maritime Military Strategy*, clearly stated that India's area of interest extends from the north of the Arabian Sea to the South China Ses.[46] Some scholars argued that India should not worry about the development of Chinese military capabilities because India will have the confidence to establish a mature bilateral tie with China. However, India is rapidly increasing its military budget and also broadening its military deployment near the disputed border with China. Data released by the Stockholm International Peace Research Institute substantiates this view, and, according to this report, India has replaced China as the world's top arms importer.[47]

In late July 2011, while returning from a goodwill visit to Vietnam, an Indian naval ship was hailed on open radio and advised to stay out of the SCS. Although such naval incidents between China and her neighbors are not unusual, this was the first one to involve India. China's Foreign Ministry spokesperson commented: "We hope foreign countries will not get involved in the dispute. . . . For countries outside the region, we hope they will respect and support countries in the region to solve this dispute through bilateral channels. We are opposed to any country engaging in oil and gas exploration and development activities in waters under China's jurisdiction."[48] China's Defense Ministry declared that China and India are not enemies or opponents, but neighbors and partners.[49] For example, both the *CNPC* and India's

ONGC have agreed to jointly explore oil and natural gas worldwide to secure energy supplies for their fast-growing economies. According to a pact signed in 2012, the companies will jointly explore assets in countries like Myanmar, Syria, and Sudan. The companies have agreed to expand cooperation in the refining, processing, marketing, and distribution of crude oil and natural gas. They will also collaborate on the construction and operation of oil and gas pipelines worldwide. For example, ONGC is working with CNPC to transport gas from Myanmar through a pipeline from the Bay of Bengal across India into southwestern China. They are also working together in Syria as well as in Sudan, holding joint stakes in 36 production fields. Furthermore, they are venturing to build an oil pipeline from South Sudan to Kenya's East African coast in order to bypass the traditional export route through the north.[50]

Nevertheless, China's hardline approach on the SCS has increasingly worried India. In fact, China offended India by denouncing ONGC Videsh's (OVL) deal with Vietnamese firms to explore oil fields in the two offshore blocks (127 and 128) in the disputed SCS, over which China claims indisputable sovereignty. China has also forced India into a difficult situation by putting up international bidding for the same Vietnamese petroleum block that India had obtained from Vietnam for exploration. Although China issued a warning to India in 2011 regarding its exploration in Blocks 127 and 128, India was not deterred. In 2012, India's oil minister, R.P.N. Singh, declared that OVL would return Block 128 to Vietnam since exploration was not commercially viable. In response, Hanoi claimed that New Delhi has succumbed to pressure from China. However, after Vietnam agreed to give India a longer period to prove commercial viability in mid-2012, India decided to continue the joint exploration. Vietnam extended the OVL contract for hydrocarbon exploration in Block 128 in order to maintain the regional strategic balance. The same year, CNOOC came forward by opening nine blocks for exploration in waters claimed by Vietnam, including oil Block 128. Furthermore, China planned on deploying troops and building strategic projects in Pakistan-occupied Kashmir (POK). There are also unconfirmed reports of confrontation between a Chinese warship and INS Airavat in the SCS.[51] Meanwhile, China has announced that it is expanding maritime exploration of 10,000 skm of seabed in the Southwest Indian Ocean. The Indian government responded immediately stating that its cooperation with Vietnam or any other country is within international laws and conventions and that India's cooperation with Vietnam in the area of energy is especially important. Indian Foreign Secretary Nirupama Rao, while addressing the National Maritime Foundation in 2011, reaffirmed the importance of the SCS as a shipping route and stated that India will support its freedom of navigation in sea-lanes. She added that Indian companies have already invested heavily in that region and will further expand their operations.[52]

Jaswant Singh even commented that China focuses on strategic encircle-ment or "wei qui." This is the oldest board game in China and as the name entails it's a game of encirclement. In other words, it is the seizure and maneuvering of strategic positions. What China did in the SCS region is a game of protracted undertaking or creeping initiatives over the decade. This is the reason that China's activity in Pakistan and Myanmar, the expansion of China's port agreements in the Indian Ocean (the so-called "string of pearls"), and heightened Chinese naval activity in the Indian Ocean has been perceived as potential threats to India's security. Ever since India's border war defeat with China in 1960, India has viewed China with deep-seated distrust. Therefore, any significant move by the Dragon made in the region would certainly bother the Elephant. Despite this mistrust, China looks for a win-win model while developing economic and trade relations with its neighbors, including India. Now, the question remains whether India will try to play smaller neighboring nations against China in order to contain China's growing clout in the region. China's assertiveness in the SCS has prompted India to declare that the disputed sea is in fact open sea, the prop-erty of the world. Although Indian naval ships frequently visit the Southeast Asian countries' ports and the SCS, cooperation with regard to nontraditional threats, like drug-trafficking, human-trafficking, and maritime terrorism, is still inadequate.

The ASEAN countries collaborated with India on other issues, for exam-ple, missile technology, radar systems, and defense component systems. India is also willing to sell Brahmos missiles to Southeast Asian countries.[53] As we have seen, India is keen on strengthening its maritime capabilities, given China's pursuit of a powerful blue water navy. Delhi views this not only as a threat to key shipping routes in the Indian Ocean but also to Indian energy assets in the SCS. Even as they compete, China is currently seeking to strengthen its ties with India, and India has also expressed its desire to improve bilateral ties with China in the twenty-first century.[54] India may not join the U.S. bandwagon to counter China; however, it will certainly develop its own muscle to effectively control the IOR. India has its trump card, the Indian Naval Ship *Satpura* (Shivalik class frigate) or Vikramaditya (aircraft carrier), to exert its influence both over the Indian Ocean and the Asia-Pacific region.

China views India's rise, overall, as a positive development that promotes China's own core interests and strategic objectives more than it threatens or challenges them. Enhanced cooperation with a rising India allows Beijing to avoid a potentially costly confrontation that would harm the growth of both countries, block the formation of a close U.S.–India relationship, and reduce the overall influence of the United States in the region. China's strategy toward a rising India combines engagement with deterrence. China is thus pursuing comprehensive political, economic, and international engagement with India to advance its broader strategic objectives. Conversely, China is seeking to deter India from undermining Chinese interests by withholding cooperation and maintaining its policies on specific issues, such as its ties with Pakistan.[55] India has traditionally followed the game of "chaupad" (four sides) or "shatranj" (chess), concentrating on contest, conquest, and subjugation. On the other hand, as mentioned earlier, China follows *wei qui*. After all, as advised by Sun Tzu, "Ultimate excellence lies . . . not in winning every battle, but in defeating the enemy, without ever fighting."[56]

Since 2000, there has been a rapid expansion of the Indian navy's area of operations into the SCS.[57] This move has had a major impact on the naval balance of power in the SCS and on the development of both bilateral and multilateral military relationships in the region. A great power in South Asia, India has always viewed the Indian Ocean as being within its sphere of influence. India has also started to develop long-range naval operations and exert control over five strategic channels: the Suez Canal, the Bab el Mandeb, the Strait of Hormuz, the Strait of Malacca, and the Sunda Strait. This has marked the beginning of its "southern forwarding strategy."[58] As a part of this strategy, the Indian navy has been expanding operations into the SCS and the Pacific Rim in the east, toward the Red Sea and the Suez Canal bordering the Mediterranean in the west, south to the southern edge of the Indian Ocean, and potentially even around the Cape of Good Hope into the Atlantic. India is also planning to attach a carrier group to its Eastern Region and Western Region fleets and to the Far East Naval Command located in the Andaman Islands. This would give India one of the largest carrier fleets in the world and would significantly improve its ability to project naval power over long distances.[59] India has also held joint military and antipiracy exercises in the SCS with countries like Vietnam, South Korea, and Japan.[60]

According to Australia's "Defense White Paper," Australia too is sufficiently unsettled by China's military transformation and modernization to embark on its most expensive procurement program, which involves the acquisition of 12 submarines, new Air Warfare Destroyers and frigates, cruise missiles, and 100 Joint Strike Fighters.[61] The *Defending Australia in the Asia Pacific Century: Force 2030* commented:

> We would be concerned about the emergence of a security environment dominated by any regional power, or powers, not committed to the same-shared goals. It would be in our strategic interests in the decades ahead that no power in the Asia-Pacific region would be able to coerce or intimidate others in the region through the employment of force, or through the implied threat of force, without being deterred, checked or, if necessary, defeated by the political, economic or military responses of others in the region.[62]

Australia acts as the quintessential "status quo power"[63] and wants its relationships with Asian nations to remain balanced amidst growing economic
integration with China, on the one hand, and its security dependence on the
United States, on the other.[64] A U.S. Defense Department paper, *China's
Military and Security Developments—2011*, argued that China's near-sea
politics has seriously disturbed not only India but also other countries like
Japan, Australia, the United States, and the ASEAN countries.[65] A recent
statement made by China has added tension in the region: "We should not
leave the world with the impression that China is only focused on economic
development, nor should we pursue the reputation of being a peaceful
power."[66] This position was not consistent with China's earlier white paper on
"China's Peaceful Development," which argued that China's key to success
was mutual economic dependence across the Pacific and a good-neighbor
policy.[67] However, things have tended in the opposite direction so far. China
has pushed its neighbors away so much so that they have already invited
the United States in the region. However, as Surin Pitsuwan, the Secretary-
General of ASEAN, commented, "The U.S.–China rivalry is certain to play
out in ASEAN; of course nobody in Southeast Asia wants to choose between
the United States and China."[68]

By 2000, the United States had switched from a policy of "active neutral-
ity" to one of "active concern" in the SCS. During the Fifteenth ASEAN–U.S.
Dialogue, which was held on May 24–25, 2000, in Kuala Lumpur, the United
States pointed out that the SCS remained an area of potential conflict.[69] The
September 11 terrorist attack provided several opportunities for the United
States to improve its relationship with other Southeast Asian countries.
For example, Vietnam and the United States increased mutual discussions
about their security relations. Moreover, on December 10, 2001, the U.S.–
Vietnam Bilateral Trade Agreement went into effect. On May 14, 2002, a
U.S.–Malaysia Anti-Terrorism Pact was concluded in Washington, whereby
the two countries pledged to increase cooperation in the areas of defense,
intelligence, border control, transportation, and law enforcement. Furthermore, Malaysia gave the United States access to its intelligence, and the
number of U.S. flights over the Malaysian-controlled airspace also increased
dramatically. The then Defense Secretary Rumsfeld stated that the United
States was very impressed with "the extent to which Malaysia is a cooperat-
ing partner in the global war on terrorism."[70] At a roundtable held in Hanoi in
2002, Admiral Dennis C. Blair, the Commander-in-Chief of U.S. forces in the
Pacific (CINCPAC), commented that he "had discussed with Vietnam's top
officials the possibilities for more participation by Vietnam in . . . regional
military activities."[71] The United States invited Vietnam to observe the Cobra
Gold regional military exercise for peacekeeping operations in the Asia-
Pacific region. Even Singapore supported the war on terror immediately after

the 9/11 attacks, allowing U.S. aircrafts to use its airfields and increasing the protection of vital shipping in the Strait of Malacca. Although Singapore maintains a strong relationship with Beijing, it remains an important post for the U.S. military presence in Asia.[72]

Information sharing between Singapore, Malaysia, Philippines, Thailand, and the United States provided unprecedented insight into the Al-Qaida networks in this region. Thailand coordinated fully with the United States in combating terrorism by granting blanket permission to U.S. planes to fly over the country and allowing U.S. refueling and support aircraft to land at airbases in Thailand. The first Thai–U.S. antiterrorist exercise, code-named *Known Warrior*, was started in August 2002.[73] The Japanese MSDF operation in the Indian Ocean that sailed through the SCS to support the U.S.-led war against terrorism was also a key development in Japanese security policy since World War II. Furthermore, U.S.–Indian military relations have expanded since the September 11 terrorist attacks, and India offered rapid and valuable assistance to the United States in conducting military operations in Afghanistan. The primary areas of cooperation between New Delhi and Washington have been peacekeeping, counterterrorism, special operations training, and naval activities.

Against the backdrop of the recent defiant rocket launch by North Korea and Suu Kyi's recent victory in parliamentary by polls, India and the United States are holding new dialogues on issues related to East Asia. The former U.S. Secretary of Defense Leon Panetta's pledge to deploy 60 percent of U.S. naval assets to the Asia-Pacific in the next few years has raised strong concerns in China. Furthermore, Panetta declared recently that in spite of the Pentagon budget cut, the United States would maintain its "force projection" in this region as China expands its military presence. China calls the United States the "sneaky troublemaker."[74] Since the summer of 2010, the Obama administration has clearly shown their initiatives through various diplomatic and military engagements in the SCS. At the 2010 ASEAN Regional Forum (ARF), the United States has made it clear about their credibility of the administrations East Asian rebalancing strategy.

Former U.S. Secretary of State Hillary Clinton had a hard time convincing the Chinese regarding U.S. intentions about containment. In fact it was hard to show the U.S. objective was still *rebalance* in the region. In 2011, President Obama declared the Asia-Pacific region, including the SCS, an area of utmost priority for the U.S. foreign policy.[75] In fact, the United States has started relocating its navy and marines to countries like Australia and Singapore. U.S. bilateral and multilateral cooperation on maritime security was leveraged in ways that can help ensure and legitimize its continuing military presence in East Asia.[76] It is clear that military clashes would be bad for all countries in the region involved, but it remains highly improbable that

China will waive its right to protect its core interest with military means.[77] As Friedman comments: "Each one of China's neighbors is eager to have a picture of their president standing with Secretary Clinton or President Obama—with the unspoken caption that reads: 'Honestly, China, we don't want to throttle you. We don't want an Asian cold war. We just want to trade and be on good terms. But, please, stay between the white lines. Don't even think about parking in my space because, if you do, I have this friend from Washington, and he's really big. . . . And he's got his own tow truck.'"[78]

Be that as it may, the steady expansion of China's maritime reconnaissance strike is creating "no-go zones" in the Western Pacific, gradually eroding the United States's military power projection into a region of long-standing vital interest.[79] Since coming to power, the Obama administration has actively promoted the vision of a tougher China and has been clear about its intentions to restore U.S. strategic importance in Asia. In the words of Sun Tzu, China is acquiring the means to "win without fighting" and is trying to establish itself as Asia's dominant power by undermining the credibility of the United States's security guarantees and eventually easing it out of the region.[80] As Eric McVadon comments, "'The PLAN' is arguably the only one in today's world that the U.S. Navy must deter or be able to defeat, and also a navy that under different circumstances could become a high-seas partner."[81] In fact, the PLAN has conducted several serious naval exercises, including those with the *Jiaolong*,[82] an amphibious deep-sea submersible, in November 2010. This demonstrates PLA's growing ability to seize islands and project military power far beyond its shores. The manned *Jiaolong* submersible undertook a deep-sea dive mission in the SCS in 2013. China is accelerating its deep-sea research by setting up a national deep-sea support base in Qingdao and building a new mother vessel for *Jiaolong* to succeed *Xiangyanghong-9*.[83] These projects were supposed to be completed within the next few years. China eventually plans to build a deep-sea station where submersibles can dock undersea and oceanauts can stay for work. The PLA feels it is also right for China to increase its national defense spending and modernize its military in response to the growing international criminal and terrorist activities.

Washington is placing marines in the northern Australian port city of Darwin and also, as explained above, increasing its military relations with Vietnam. Panetta's visit to Vietnam and a tour of the Cam Ranh Bay in 2012 made it clear that the use of the harbor is important to the Pentagon since it is moving more ships to Asia.[84] The Eagle has clearly stated that it has no intention of leaving the area and that it is rather trying to strengthen its legal hand so that its navy can be assured the freedom of navigation that UNCLOS recognizes beyond any nation's territorial limit of 12 nms. The United States has additionally stressed that freedom of navigation in the SCS should not be interrupted due to its strategic and economic interests in the Asia-Pacific region. In May 2008, during the Shangri-La Dialogue in Singapore, Former U.S. Defense Secretary Robert Gates described the United States as "a Pacific nation with an enduring role in East Asia."[85] Former U.S. Secretary of State Hillary Clinton stated at the ARF meeting in Hanoi in July 2010 that, "[T] he U.S. has national interest in freedom of navigation, open access to Asia's maritime commons, and respect for international law in the South China Sea."[86] In fact Hillary's reference to the SCS as international waters sparked controversy.[87] As a result, China warned the United States to stay out of this matter and not to interfere in regional territorial disputes.[88] On another front, the U.S. Congress has mandated the Department of Defense (through the Taiwan Relations Act) to sell defensive weapons to Taiwan and instructed the U.S. Pacific Command to maintain the capability to prevail in a conflict with China over Taiwan.[89]

Ambassador Susan Rice in November 2013 delivered an address about the U.S. rebalance strategies in Asia. She had stressed on the fact that the rebalance strategy will not only be multidimensional in nature but will also remain as a cornerstone of the Obama Administration's foreign policy. Besides, by 2020, 60 percent of the U.S. fleet will be based in the Pacific, and the Pacific Command will gain more of America's most cutting-edge capabilities.[90]

No matter how many hotspots emerge elsewhere, we will continue to deepen our enduring commitment to this critical region. Our friends in Asia deserve and will continue to get our highest-level attention.[91]

Again in 2014, Secretary Kerry made it clear with his speech at the East West Center in Honolulu, that the Obama administration's goal is to achieve a rules-based regional order:

> Important opportunities can and should be realized through a rules-based regional order, a stable regional order on common rules and norms of behavior that are reinforced by institutions. And that's what holds the greatest potential for all of us for making progress. We support this approach, frankly, because it encourages cooperative behavior. It fosters regional integration. It ensures that all countries, big and small—and the small part is really important—that they have a say in how we work together on shared challenges. I want you to know that the United States is deeply committed to realizing this vision.[92]

General Xu Caihou, Vice Chairman of China's Central Military Commission (CMC), met with the U.S. National Security Advisor, Chairman of the Joint Chiefs of Staff, and the Deputy Secretary of State and signed an agreement on seven important issues. The issues cover promoting high-level visits, enhancing cooperation in the area of humanitarian assistance and disaster relief, deepening military medical cooperation, expanding exchanges between armies of the two nations, enhancing the program of midgrade and junior officer exchanges, promoting cultural and sports exchanges between the two militaries, and invigorating the existing diplomatic and consultative mechanisms to improve maritime operational safety. However, it was also clear at the meeting that U.S.–China military relations still have a long way to go. In fact there are few major obstacles that are harming bilateral relations between the two nations. The first and foremost obstacle is the U.S.–Taiwan military relationship, which again is a matter of core interest to China. Second is the intrusion of U.S. military aircrafts and ships into China's maritime EEZ. The third is that a few U.S. policies, like the 2000 Defense Authorization Act, restrict the development of the military relationship between China and the U.S. Finally, the lack of trust the United States has in China.[93] According to Valencia, "American forces are testing China's ability to detect foreign vessels and aircraft by tickling their radar stations, interfering with ship to shore communications and attempting to detect how Chinese submarines enter and leave their bases."[94] According to China, "Such activities are a form of battlefield preparation, which are prohibited by Chinese domestic law."[95] Ji Guoxing regards such activities as counter to UNCLOS article 301, which stipulates that parties shall refrain from threatening the sovereignty of any state when exercising their rights at sea.[96]

China is increasingly becoming concerned about the neo-interventionism and neo-gunboat policy of other major powers, and Washington's involvement in particular has created much alarm and trepidation within China. Chinese leaders began advocating "peaceful rise" as soon as they realized that Beijing's hard power stance was widely mistrusted. Beijing has called upon other nations in Asia to abandon their alliances with the United States and has warned against foreign intervention in the SCS. However, this strategy seems to have backfired.[97] China has also warned Australia about its decision to strengthen military ties with the United States while continuing Australia's economic dependency on China. The issue has become further complicated with the growing importance of the city of Zhanjiang, which is China's main naval command center for ships and also the export destination for tons of Australian iron ore.[98]

The 2007 *A Cooperative Strategy for 21st Century Sea power views the regions of the* Western Pacific and the Indian Ocean (including the Persian Gulf) as the central theatres for the exercise of hard U.S. naval power. The SCS, which lies between the two theaters, of course, is a gateway both for merchant shipping and for navies.[99] The report states that through persistent presence, and operational flexibility, the United States will accomplish several key strategic imperatives. U.S. maritime forces will have the combat power to limit regional conflict, deter major power war, foster and sustain cooperative relationships with an expanding set of international partners, and prevent crises.[100] The United States has even discussed conducting operations in the

Himalayan region as a humanitarian mission to search for the remains of U.S. pilots listed as missing after World War II.[101] The operation will be held in Arunachal Pradesh, disputed by China, which suspects that the mission is not purely humanitarian. The United States took a seat at the East Asian Summit and engaged in negotiations to create a Trans–Pacific Partnership Free Trade Agreement (TPP) without China. It may still be that India's growing involvement with Vietnam or its moves in the SCS will act as a counterweight to China's activities and support in Bangladesh, Myanmar, and Pakistan. Henry Kissinger, in his book, *On China*, stated that China's approach to world order is dissimilar to the Western system of a "balance of power diplomacy, primarily because China has never engaged in sustained contact with another . . . on the basis of the concept of the sovereign equality of nations."[102] The question remains whether the Eagle and the Elephant along with other nations contend with the Dragon's assertiveness by following Sun Tzu's advice to "contain an adversary through the leverage of converting the neighborhood of that adversary into hostiles"?[103]

The landmark defense deal between the United States and India is a sign of the rapidly growing defense and security ties between New Delhi and Washington following 9/11. At the same time, India is improving its relationship with the ASEAN member states and has signed a 14-article agreement for collaboration with Vietnam. The United States is concerned with the fact that naval confrontation between China and India in the SCS could affect its national interests with respect to the maintenance of peace and stability in the region and the free passage of U.S. ships through the SCS. Yet the United States also views the expansion of Indian power in the SCS as a positive step to contain China's steadily increasing naval presence in the region.

The recent report released by the Center for New American Security, "*Preserving the Rules: Countering Coercion in Maritime Asia*,"[104] proposed adopting cost-imposing measures to address China's reclamation in the SCS region. In fact several recommendations were made such as mobilizing regional and international opinion when states use coercion; mobilizing support for positive efforts to foster a rules-based order and so on. to mellow down tensions creeping in the region. Although the United States and China have agreed to take a "substantive leap" with regard to military-to-military cooperation,[105] scholars also talk about a "C-shaped ring of encirclement by China."[106] Others even argue that the United States is organizing an "Asian version of NATO" against China. Following Vannarith, the question is whether the U.S. military presence in East Asia is a part of U.S. strategy to counterbalance China's efforts in creating the *Energy Silk Road* or to complete the geographical containment of China.[107]

The United States could strengthen its own position by becoming a party to the UN Convention on the Law of the Sea. As General Xu recognized, various obstacles stand in the way of improved security relations with China. First is the U.S. sale of arms to Taiwan, followed by the intense spy and patrol activities of U.S. aircraft and ships in the South and East China Sea. Another is the 2000 National Defense Authorization Act, which set conditions and limits on U.S. military contacts with China.[108]

China's "string of pearls" strategy has become an important one in terms of expanding its power.[109] If leaders of other South Asian states contemplate militarizing some of these "pearls," it would be difficult for Beijing to convince them that hosting PLAN bases is in their best interests. As "swing players" in an emerging Indo-Pacific "great game," the littoral states of the Indian Ocean will probably prefer not to align but rather oscillate between Beijing, New Delhi, and Washington.[110]

BEIJING: THE SOUTH CHINA SEA AND THE ARCTIC STRATEGY

As strategic questions are being raised about the SCS dispute, another issue of growing importance is China's Arctic strategy. China has become increasingly serious about the consequences of melting ice in the Arctic Ocean due to climate change. However, Beijing's collaborative actions and behavior in the Arctic is way different from that of the SCS. The melting of the Arctic ice would mean greater use of the Northeast Passage, which would in turn decrease dependence on the Malacca Strait. Although new commercial opportunities for cooperation will arise as a result of an ice-free Arctic, at the same time there is a significant likelihood that tension and miscalculation will characterize this region much as it has in the SCS. In fact, the U.S. Navy Task Force on Climate Change completed its latest assessment of the Arctic region and reported that the developing situation in the Arctic resembles that which is unfolding in the SCS.

China views this unique Arctic opportunity as potentially beneficial for its international trade and shipping, with a major impact on China's future economy. China has therefore sought observer status at the Arctic Council that looks at various Arctic issues, including shipping. The opening of the Arctic means more available routes that have a lower risk of piracy, and this would certainly be helpful for China whose seven ports are on the list of the world's top 20 container terminals.[111] At the 2009 Arctic Forum in Norway, Hu stated: "Arctic countries should protect the balance between the interests of states with shorelines in the Arctic Ocean and the shared interests of the international community in settling territorial claims."[112] China's State Oceanic Administration declared in 2010 that, "[T] he Arctic is the inherited wealth of all humankind. . . . The Arctic Ocean is not the backyard of any country and is not the private property of the Arctic Ocean littoral states. Under the framework of international law, every country in the world has an equal right to exploit the Arctic Ocean."[113] Interestingly, China's assertive position regarding other countries' sovereignty claims in the Arctic might undermine its own position in contested areas like the SCS. China's movements in the Arctic lie in stark contrast to that of the SCS. While China has an open mind and maintains a cooperative behavior in the Arctic, it nurtures a very secluded and disjointed behavior in the SCS. It is clear that China will at least have to learn how to *share and bear* when it comes to the SCS region.

The question remains whether China is trying to initiate a new version of a Greater East Asia Co-Prosperity Sphere that was the intention of imperial Japan during 1940. According to the "Co-Prosperity Sphere" concept at that time, supplying regional raw materials and energy resources would facilitate Japan's control over the access of other countries to vital areas and commercial routes and also ensure the nation's own self-sufficiency. Likewise, China is now asserting its territorial and maritime claims in the East and SCS, maintaining its long-standing claim over the Taiwan Strait, making claims in the Indian Ocean, and implementing a "string of pearls" strategy. China might learn some lessons from Norway's earlier claims over Svalbard. According to the 1920 Spitsbergen Treaty, Norway was granted sovereignty over the Spitsbergen archipelago, or Svalbard. However, the treaty restricted Norway's control to some extent and Norway was obliged not to discriminate against any nation or company from the signatory states seeking to undertake maritime or mining activity on the island. In fact, Norway has never interrupted the global supply of oil, not surprisingly perhaps because it is both an oil exporter and explorer.[114] Beijing should also understand that with the melting of Arctic ice, the Northwest Passage would be used by countries to reduce shipping time between Europe and Asia. As the *Japan Times* commented, the Northern Sea Route (NSR) will force nations to reassess their maritime strategies.[115] In fact the Arctic states of Europe could perhaps serve as a role model for Asia.

There are rumors that Beijing is investing money in developing advanced air defenses, submarines, antisatellite weapons, and antiship missiles, and use them to deny other countries access to the SCS. Furthermore, China has recently announced new rules allowing for the interception of ships in the SCS, which has raised serious alarm across Asia.[116] If China were to fully enforce these new rules beyond the 12-nm zones, it would represent a significant threat to all countries concerned.[117] In 2013, Beijing even published a new vertical-format map of China including 130 islands and islets in the SCS, which were not featured previously.[118] Such actions are certain to increase tensions all the more in the region. Moreover, China's activities in the Maldives, which are viewed by the Maldives as important for maintaining security in the IOR, are emerging as a new area of conflict. China is busy building ties with other island nations located on or near to India's border, like Sri Lanka, Seychelles and Mauritius. Former President Hu Jintao defined the objective of China's foreign policy as to "jointly construct a harmonious world," and invokes the cultural idea of "all under heaven," or Tianxia.[119] Perhaps, if his statement is true, then China will not undertake aggressive actions in the SCS to advance its territorial claims and meet its rapidly increasing energy demands.

For its part, the Beijing-based *Global Times* stated that regional stability would be difficult to maintain if the Southeast Asian states allow themselves to be controlled by the United States. While Australia appears to favor China's bilateral approach in resolving the SCS disputes; Singapore, Thailand, and the Philippines seem to prefer the current arrangement of placing the matter on ASEAN's agenda.[120] If China is convinced that the United States is stealthily trying to draw ASEAN or some of its members together with Australia, Japan, and South Korea into a soft alliance to constrain China, then the world can only expect even greater rivalry and tension in the years ahead. Consider, for instance, former U.S. Secretary of Defense Robert Gates's remarks in 2010:

> We have a national interest in freedom of navigation, in unimpeded economic development and commerce in respect for international law, the United States has always exercised our rights and supported the rights of others to transit through and operate in international waters. This will not change, nor will our commitment to engage in activities and exercises together with our allies and partners.[121]

However, at the February 2015 meeting of the United Nations Security Council (UNSC), Beijing's Foreign Minister while conducting its foreign policy strategies has mentioned their intentions to maintain peace and not conflict, cooperation and not confrontation, justice and not hegemony, and a win-win approach as opposed to a zero-sum approach. However, the biggest concern still remains whether the *rojo-phobia* will continue to exist and whether Beijing will be able to deliver its peaceful intention to the international community.

The following chapter will discuss the role of ASEAN and focus on different methods to resolve crisis in the region.

NOTES

1. Michael Klare, *Resource Wars: The New Landscape of Global Conflict* (New York: Henry Holt and Company, LLC, 2001), 109–137.

2. Kent E. Calder, "China and Japan's Simmering Rivalry," *Foreign Affairs* 8, no. 2 (2006):129–139.

3. Mikkel E. Herberg, "Asia's Energy Insecurity: Cooperation or Conflict?", in *Strategic Asia 2004–05: Confronting Terrorism in the Pursuit of Power*, ed. A. J. Tellis and M. Wills (Seattle, WA: The National Bureau of Asian Research, 2005).

4. Mark J. Valencia, "The South China Sea: Back to the Future?" *Global Asia: A Journal of the East Asia Foundation* (December 2010), http://www.globalasia.org/V5N4_Winter_2010/Mark_J_Valencia.html.

5. Andy Yee, "China and its Territorial Disputes: One Approach Does Not Fit All," *East Asia Forum*, January 10, 2011, http://www.eastasiaforum.org/2011/01/20/china-and-its-territorial-disputes-one-approach-does-not-fit-all/.

6. Carlyle Thayer, "Recent Developments in the South China Sea: Implications for Peace, Stability and Cooperation in the Region," in *The South China Sea: Cooperation For Regional Security and Development: Proceedings of the International Workshop Co-organized by the Diplomatic Academy of Vietnam and the Vietnam Lawyers' Association*, ed. Thuy, Tran Truong, 125–38 (Hanoi: Diplomatic Academy of Vietnam, November 2009), http://nghiencuubiendong.vn/en/datbase-on-south-china-sea-study/doc_details/36-the-south-china-sea-cooperation-for-regional-security-and-development.

7. Carlyle Thayer, "China's New Wave of Aggressive Assertiveness in the South China Sea" (online paper, Center for Strategic and International Studies, Washington, DC, June 30, 2011), http://csis.org/publication/chinas-new-wave-aggressive-assertiveness-south-china-sea.

8. Ibid.

9. Saibal Dasgupta, "Vietnamese Threat to China, from the Sea?" *Times of India*, June 12, 2011, http://articles.timesofindia.indiatimes.com/2011-06-12/china/29649924_1_south-china-sea-chinese-fishermen-ammunition-drill.

10. Thayer, "China's New Wave of Aggressive Assertiveness in the South China Sea," 19.

11. Ibid.

12. Ibid.

13. Ibid.

14. Jens Kastner, "Taiwan Circling South China Sea Bait," *Asia Times Online*, June 12, 2012, http://centurychina.com/plaboard/posts/3907063.shtml.

15. Sarah Serizawn, "China's Military Modernization and Implications for Northeast Asia: An Interview with Christopher W. Hughes," *National Bureau of Asian Research*, August 2, 2012, http://www.nbr.org/research/activity.aspx?id=266.

16. Ibid.

17. Ibid.

18. Carol J. Williams, "China-U.S. Power Play at Core of East Asian Island Disputes," *Los Angeles Times*, September 12, 2012, http://latimesblogs.latimes.com/world_now/2012/09/china-us-power-play-at-core-of-east-asian-island-disputes.html; Frank Ching, "East Asia's Free for All-Territorial Disputes with South Korea and China Over Islets Reveal Rising Nationalism, Japan's Weakness," *Yale Global*, August 30, 2012, http://yaleglobal.yale.edu/content/east-asias-free-all; Mark McDonald,

"East Asia's Sea Disputes: Scar Tissue from War Wounds," *IHT Rendezvous*, August 16, 2012, http://rendezvous.blogs.nytimes.com/2012/08/16/east-asias-sea-disputes-scar-tissue-from-war-wounds/; Global Times, "China opposes application of U.S.-Japan security treaty to Diaoyu Islands," August 26, 2012, http://www.globaltimes.cn/content/729056.shtml.

19. BBC News Asia, "South Korea's Lee Myung-bak Visits Disputed Islands," August 10, 2012.

20. David Philling, "Asia's Quiet Anger with 'Big, Bad' China," *Financial Times*, June 2, 2011, http://www.ft.com/intl/cms/s/0/da3396b6-8c81-11e0-883f-00144fe-ab49a.html.

21. Carlyle Thayer, "Is the Philippines an Orphan?" *The Diplomat*, May 2, 2012, http://thediplomat.com/2012/05/02/is-the-philippines-an-orphan/.

22. Stanley Weiss, "Rowing between two reefs," *New York Times*, August 30, 2010, http://www.nytimes.com/2010/08/31/opinion/31iht-edweiss.html?gwh=931A8 D84C6764E888EE1735B33F8ED7D.

23. Xinhua, english.news.cn, "Renaming of Area in South China Sea will not Affect China's Sovereignty," September 13, 2012. http://news.xinhuanet.com/english/china/2012-09/13/c_131848692.htm.

24. Thayer, "China's New Wave of Aggressive Assertiveness in the South China Sea," 2011.

25. Ibid.

26. Ibid.

27. Ibid.

28. Carlyle A. Thayer, "Standoff in the South China Sea Scarborough Shoal Standoff Reveals Blunt Edge of China's Peaceful Rise," *Yale Global*, June 12, 2012. http://yaleglobal.yale.edu/content/standoff-south-china-sea.

29. Ibid.

30. Jerry Esplanada, "China Not Pulling out 7 Vessels around Scarborough Shoal," *Philippine Daily Inquirer*, June 19, 2012.

31. Thayer, "Standoff in the South China Sea Scarborough Shoal Standoff Reveals Blunt Edge of China's Peaceful Rise."

32. Times of India, "China to Deploy Drones to Conduct Maritime Surveillance," August 29, 2012, http://articles.timesofindia.indiatimes.com/2012-08-29/china/33475416_1_maritime-disputes-drones-state-oceanic-administration.

33. Jane Perlez, "Beijing Exhibiting New Assertiveness in South China Sea," *New York Times*, May 31, 2012, http://www.nytimes.com/2012/06/01/world/asia/beijing-projects-power-in-strategic-south-china-sea.html?pagewanted=all&_r=0.

34. GMA News Online, "China to Build Communication Network Covering South China Sea islets," September 14, 2012. http://www.gmanetwork.com/news/story/273945/news/world/china-to-build-communication-network-covering-south-china-sea-islets.

35. Global Times, "Don't Take Peaceful Approach for Granted," October 25, 2011. http://www.globaltimes.cn/.

36. Reuters "China Tests Troubled Waters with $1 bln Rig for South China Sea," June 21, 2012, http://www.reuters.com/article/2012/06/21/us-china-southchinasea-idUSBRE85K03Y20120621.

37. John Bradford, "The Growing Prospects For Maritime Security Cooperation in Southeast Asia," *Naval war College Review* 58, no. 3 (Summer 2005): 63–86.

38. Srikanth Kondapalli, "The Chinese Military Eyes South Asia," in *Shaping China's Security Environment: The Role of The People's Liberation Army Andrew*, ed. Scobell and Larry Wortzel (Strategic Studies Institute, U.S. Army War College, 2006): 198–282.

39. Eric S. Morse, "Geopolitics in the South China Sea and Indian Ocean Region: Tiny Ripples or Shifting Tides?" National Strategy Forum Review Blog, August 30, 2010. www.nationalstrategy.com

40. Kondapalli, "The Chinese Military Eyes South Asia."

41. Ma Liyao, "Indian report points to China's growing military capabilities," *China Daily*, March 24, 2011, http://www.chinadaily.com.cn/cndy/2011-03/24/content_12218839.htm.

42. Kondapalli, "The Chinese Military Eyes South Asia."

43. Ibid., 198.

44. Ibid.

45. Ibid.

46. Amit Singh, "South China Sea Dispute And India," *National Maritime Foundation*, June 20, 2012.

47. Reuters, "India Army Chief Wary of Growing China Military," July 4, 2004. http://www.reuters.com/article/2012/06/21/us-china-southchinasea-idUSBRE85K03Y20120621.

48. Ananth Krishnan, "China Warns India in South China Sea Exploration Projects," *The Hindu*, September 15, 2011. http://www.thehindu.com/news/international/article2455647.ece.

49. Jaswant Singh, "Asia's Giants Colliding at Sea?" Project Syndicate, October 24, 2011. http://www.project-syndicate.org/commentary/asia-s-giants-colliding-at-sea.

50. Sharma Rakesh, "Oil Firms in China And India Pull Closer," *Wall Street Journal*, June 19, 2012. http://online.wsj.com/article/SB10001424052702303836404577476090216555460.html.

51. Singh, "South China Sea Dispute And India"; Harsh V. Pant, "South China Sea: New Arena of Sino-Indian Rivalry: China Ignores India's Exploration, Puts Vietnam's Oil Block up for Global Bid," *Yale Global*, August 2, 2012. http://yaleglobal.yale.edu/content/south-china-sea-new-arena-sino-indian-rivalry.

52. Singh, "Asia's Giants Colliding at Sea?"

53. Singh, "South China Sea Dispute And India."

54. S. M. krishna, "Ties with China Priority of India's Foreign Policy," *Daily News and Analysis*, June 6, 2012. http://www.dnaindia.com/india/report_ties-with-china-priority-of-india-s-foreign-policy-sm-krishna_1699011.

55. Ashley J. Tellis, Travis Tanner and Jessica Keough, eds. *Strategic Asia 2011–12: Asia Responds to Its Rising Powers—China and India* (Seattle: WA National Bureau of Asian Research, 2011).

56. Singh, "Asia's Giants Colliding at Sea?"

57. Asia Times, "India Challenges China in South China Sea," April 26, 2000. http://www.atimes.com/ind-pak/BD27Df01.html.

58. Economic Times "South China Sea an Area of 'Significant Concern': Indian Navy Chief," November 17, 2011. http://articles.economictimes.indiatimes.com/2011-11-17/news/30410113_1_south-china-sea-indian-navy-territorial-disputes.

59. Yann-Huei Song, "The Overall Situation in the South China Sea in the New Millennium: Before and After the September 11 Terrorist Attacks," *Ocean Development and International Law* 34 (2003): 229–277.

60. Ibid.

61. John Wong, "New Dimensions in China-ASEAN Relations," in *China-ASEAN Relations: Economic and Legal Dimensions*, ed. John Wong (Hackensack, NJ: World Scientific Publishing Company, 2006).

62. Ibid.

63. Hugh White, "Power Shift: Australia's Future between Washington and Beijing," *Quarterly Essay* 39 (September 2010), http://www.quarterlyessay.com/issue/power-shift-australia%E2%80%99s-future-between-washington-and-beijing.

64. Robert Kaplan, "The South China Sea Is the Future of Conflict," *Foreign Policy* 188 (October 2011): 1–8.

65. Bhaskar Roy, "China's Near Sea Policy Provoking Regional Instability—Analysis," *Eurasia Review*, September 20, 2012, http://www.eurasiareview.com/20092011-china%E2%80%99s-near-sea-policy-provoking-regional-instability-analysis/.

66. Ibid.

67. Stein Tonnesson, "China's Boomerang Diplomacy: China's Treatment of East Asian Neighbors Hits Back and Undermines its Peaceful Development," *Yale Global* (November 2012).

68. Ibid.

69. Song, "The Overall Situation in the South China Sea in the New Millennium."

70. Ibid.

71. Ibid.

72. Jane Perlez, "Singaporean Tells China U.S. Is Not in Decline," *New York Times*, September 6, 2012. http://www.nytimes.com/2012/09/07/world/asia/singapores-prime-minister-warns-china-on-view-of-us.html.

73. Song, "The Overall Situation in the South China Sea in the New Millennium."

74. Kathrin Hille, "Clinton Struggles to Soothe Beijing Fears," Financial Times, September 5, 2012. http://www.ft.com/cms/s/0/9b296eec-f728-11e1-8e9e-00144feabdc0.html.

75. Boris Volkhonsky, "U.S. Policy in the South China Sea," *Voice of Russia*, June 9, 2012. http://english.ruvr.ru/2012_06_09/77629409/.

76. Aileen S. P. Baviera, "Territorial Disputes in East Asia: Proxies for China-US Strategic Competition?" *East Asia Forum*, November 27, 2010. http://www.eastasiaforum.org/2010/11/27/territorial-disputes-in-east-asia-proxies-for-china-us-strategic-competition/.

77. John Chan, "US-China Tensions over South China Sea," World Socialist Web Site, August 4, 2010. http://www.wsws.org/en/articles/2010/08/usch-a04.html

78. Thomas Friedman, "Containment-Lite," *New York Times*, November 9, 2010. http://www.nytimes.com/2010/11/10/opinion/10friedman.html.

79. Jim Thomas, "China's Active Defense Strategy And Its Regional Implications," Testimony Before The U.S.-China Economic And Security Review Commission, January 2011: 1–5.

80. Arron Friedberg, "China's Challenge at Sea," *New York Times*, September 4, 2011. http://www.nytimes.com/2011/09/05/opinion/chinas-challenge-at-sea.html.

81. Marvin Taylor, "PRC Area-Denial Capabilities and American Power Projection," Prospects Blog, June 2012, http://prospectjournalblog.wordpress.com/; Elisabeh Bumiller, "U.S. to Sustain Military Power in the Pacific," *The New York Times*, October 23, 2011, http://www.nytimes.com/2011/10/24/world/asia/panetta-tells-pacific-countries-that-us-will-keep-strong-presence.html?r=0; Lisa Holland, "China Celebrates Its Growing Military Might," Yahoonews.com, August 1, 2012. http://uk.news.yahoo.com/china-celebrates-growing-military-might-074525669.html.

82. The Chinese government has been testing to launch a new submersible, in 2010 named Jiaolong, which can dive to 7,000 meters. If successful, it will be the deepest diving submersible in the world, diving deeper than the Japanese Shinaki 6500, which can dive to 6,500 meters and the American submersible Alvin, which can dive to 4,500 meters.

83. Xinhua, English.news.cn, "Xinhua Insight: China Manned Sub may Dive in South China Sea 2013," July16, 2012. http://news.xinhuanet.com/english/indepth/2012-07/16/c_131718966.htm.

84. Reuters, "China Tests Troubled Waters with $1 bln rig for South China Sea."

85. Ibid.

86. Mark Landler, Offering to Aid Talks, U.S. Challenges China on Disputed Islands, *The New York Times*, July 23, 2010. http://www.nytimes.com/2010/07/24/world/asia/24diplo.html.

87. Michael Richardson, "In Knots and Tangles Over Freedom of the Sea," *The Straits Times*, July 28, 2010, http://www.iseas.edu.sg/viewpoint/mr28jul10.pdf.

88. Andrew Jacobs, "China Warns U.S. to Stay Out of Islands Dispute," *New York Times*, July 26, 2010, http://www.nytimes.com/2010/07/27/world/asia/27china.html.

89. John Wong, "New Dimensions in China-ASEAN Relations."

90. Susan E. Rice, "America's Future in Asia," November 20, 2013, Georgetown University, http://www.whitehouse.gov/the-press-office/2013/11/21/remarks-prepared-delivery-national- security-advisor-susan-e-rice

91. Ibid.

92. Secretary of State John Kerry, "Remarks at the East West Center on the U.S. Vision for the Asia-Pacific," Honolulu, Hawaii, August 14, 2014, http://iipdigital.usembassy.gov/st/ english/texttrans/2014/08/20140814305641.html#ixzz3B3fyWzwJ

93. Ibid.

94. Ibid.

95. Ren Xiaofeng and Cheng Xizhong, "A Chinese Perspective," *Marine Policy* 29 (2005): 139–46.

96. James Manicom, "Beyond Boundary Disputes: Understanding The Nature of China's Challenge to Maritime East Asia," *Harvard Asia Quarterly* 12, no. ¾ (2011): 46–53.

97. John Garnaut, "China Warns on US-Australian Ties," *The Age*, June 7, 2012. http://www.theage.com.au/national/china-warns-on-usaustralian-ties-20120606-1zwp0.html.

98. Ibid.

99. James R. Holmes, "South China Sea Is No Black Sea," *The Diplomat*, October 5, 2011. http://thediplomat.com/2011/10/05/south-china-sea-is-no-black-sea/.

100. U.S. Marine Corps, "A Cooperative Strategy for 21st Century Sea power," October 2007, http://www.navy.mil/maritime/Maritimestrategy.pdf.

101. Boris Volkhonsky, "U.S. Policy in the South China Sea."

102. Henry Kissinger, On China (New York Penguin Press HC, 2011).

103. Ibid.

104. Nong Hong, "Face-Off in the South China Sea: Conflict or Compromise?" Asia Maritime Transparency Initiative (March 2015). See http://amti.csis.org/the-post-reclamation-scenario-in-the-south-china-sea-the-role-of-china-and-the-united-states/.

105. Song, "The Overall Situation in the South China Sea in the New Millennium."

106. Holmes, "What 'Containing China' Means."

107. Chheang Vannarith, "Asia Pacific Security Issues: Challenges and Adaptive Mechanism," *Cambodian Institute for Cooperation and Peace Policy Brief* 3 (July 2010). http://www.cicp.org.kh/download/CICP%20Policy%20brief/CICP%20Policy%20brief%20No%203.pdf.

108. Ibid.

109. Pan Chengxin, "Is the South China Sea a new 'Dangerous Ground' for US-China rivalry?" *East Asia Forum*, May 24, 2011, http://www.eastasiaforum.org/2011/05/24/is-the-south-china-sea-a-new-dangerous-ground-for-us-china-rivalry/; The "String of Pearls" term was used in an internal U.S. Department of Defense report titled Energy Futures In Asia. According to this article, "[T]he String of Pearls describes the manifestation of China's rising geopolitical influence through efforts to increase access to ports and airfields, develop special diplomatic relationships, and modernize military forces that extend from the South China Sea through the Strait of Malacca, across the Indian Ocean, and on to the Persian Gulf." See Chris Devonshire-Ellis, "China's String of Pearls Strategy," *China Briefing*, March 18, 2009. http://www.china-briefing.com/news/2009/03/18/china%E2%80%99s-string-of-pearls-strategy.html.

110. Ashley S, Townshend, "Unraveling China's 'String of Pearl,' *Yale Global*, September16, 2011. http://yaleglobal.yale.edu/content/unraveling-chinas-string-pearls.

111. Nong Hong, "The Melting Arctic and Its Impact on China's Maritime Transport," *Research in Transportation Economics* 35, no. 1 (May 2012): 50–7.

112. Caitlin Campbell, "China and the Arctic: Objectives and Obstacles," U.S.-China Economic and Security Review Commission Staff Research Report (2012), http://www.uscc.gov/researchpapers/2012/China-and-the-Arctic_Apr2012.pdf. The five Arctic littoral states are Canada, Denmark (of which Greenland is a territory), Norway, Russia, and the United States (by virtue of Alaska). An additional three countries have territory in the Arctic Circle: Finland, Iceland, and Sweden. The waters

of the Arctic Ocean are basically controlled by the eight polar states: Canada, Russia, Norway, Sweden, Finland, Iceland, the United States (via Alaska), and Denmark (via Greenland). They have set policy for the region through the Arctic Council created in 1996.

113. Ibid.

114. Parag Khanna and John Gilman, "Does Norway Hold Key to Solving South China Sea Dispute?" CNN, November 13, 2012. http://www.cnn.com/2012/11/13/opinion/khanna-south-china-sea-dispute/index.html.

115. Margaret Blunden, "Geopolitics and the Northern Sea Route," *International Affairs* 88, no. 1 (2012): 115–129.

116. Jane Perlez, "Alarm as China Issues Rules for Disputed Area," *New York Times*, December 1, 2012. http://www.nytimes.com/2012/12/02/world/asia/alarm-as-china-issues-rules-for-disputed-sea.html?r=0.

117. Sudhi Ranjan Sen, "Indian Navy will Intervene in South China Sea, if required," NDTV (India) December 3, 2012, http://www.ndtv.com/article/india/indian-navy-will-intervene-in-south-china-sea-if-required-300388.

118. Xinhua, english.news.cn, "China Publishes New Maps: South China Sea Islands Highlighted," English.cri.cn, January 11, 2013. http://news.xinhuanet.com/english/china/2013-01/11/c_132097207.htm.

119. Amitav Acharya, "Can Asia Step Up to 21st Century Leadership?" *Yale Global*, December 1, 2011. http://yaleglobal.yale.edu/content/can-asia-step-21st-century-leadership.

120. Valencia, "The South China Sea: Back to the Future?"

121. Bill Van Auken, "Pentagon Chief Asserts US National Interest in China Seas," wsws.org, October 13, 2010, http://www.wsws.org/en/articles/2010/10/gate-o13.html.

Chapter 5

The ASEAN Way

Southeast Asia minus ASEAN equals greater political instability, more widespread economic deterioration and, almost surely,
the ascendancy of expansionist forces that thrive on the weakness,
isolation, and disunity of others.

—ASEAN Secretary-General Narciso G. Reyes

BIRTH OF ASEAN

The ASEAN was established with the signing of the ASEAN Declaration on
August 8, 1967, in Bangkok, Thailand, by the foreign ministers of Indonesia,
Malaysia, the Philippines, Singapore, and Thailand. Since then, membership
has expanded to include Brunei, Myanmar, Cambodia, Laos, and Vietnam.
The declaration called for the establishment of an Association for Regional
Cooperation in Southeast Asia to be known as ASEAN. Its stated objectives
are accelerating economic growth, social progress, and cultural development
through joint endeavors and above all to promote regional peace and stability. Its founding document called for its regional member countries to respect
justice and the rule of law and adhere to the principles of the United Nations
Charter.

Additionally, ASEAN acts to promote active collaboration and mutual
assistance on matters of common interest, provide assistance to members in
the form of training and research facilities, collaborate more effectively for
the greater utilization of their agriculture and industries, promote Southeast
Asian studies, and maintain close and beneficial cooperation with existing
international and regional organizations.[1] ASEAN thus purports to represent

"the collective will of the nations of Southeast Asia to bind themselves together in friendship and cooperation and, through joint efforts and sacrifices, secure for their peoples and for posterity the blessings of peace, freedom and prosperity."[2] The two-page Bangkok Declaration contains the rationale for the establishment of ASEAN as well as its modus operandi of building on voluntary and informal arrangements toward more binding and institutionalized agreements.[3] In their relations with one another, the ASEAN member states have also adopted a few fundamental principles, contained in the 1976 Treaty of Amity and Cooperation (TAC). They are as follows:[4]

Mutual respect for the independence, sovereignty, equality, territorial integrity, and national identity of all nations;
The right of every State to lead its national existence free from external interference, subversion or coercion;
Noninterference in the internal affairs of one another;
Settlement of differences or disputes by peaceful manner;
Renunciation of the threat or use of force; and
Effective cooperation.

ASEAN is a central structure in Asia-Pacific regional institutional architecture. The establishment of ASEAN in 1967 was prompted by the outbreak of interstate disputes, like the conflict over Sabah (Malaysia vs. Philippines). ASEAN survived those early disputes and, for the first decade of its life, attempted to define and refine the concepts that formed the basis of its identity. During those early years, ASEAN member countries developed a habit of working together and resolved to keep external powers from intervening in the internal affairs of Southeast Asia. In 1971, the five ASEAN foreign ministers met in Kuala Lumpur and established the Zone of Peace, Freedom and Neutrality (ZOPFAN), also known as the Kuala Lumpur Declaration. In the declaration, the parties publicly stated their intention to keep Southeast Asia free from outside interference. The first multilateral treaty that served as a part of the code of conduct for SCS states was the TAC, mentioned above, which only governed relations among the member states of ASEAN.[5] The Second Protocol to TAC enabled non–Southeast Asian states to become parties to TAC as a demonstration of their commitment to friendly and constructive relations. By the early 1990s, ASEAN members claimed that their organization was one of the most successful experiments in regional cooperation in the developing world. At the heart of this claim was ASEAN's role in moderating intra-regional conflicts and significantly reducing the likelihood of war. Although ASEAN's diplomatic initiative led to the Paris Peace Agreement on Cambodia in 1991,[6] however ASEAN's credibility and the so-called ASEAN way has frequently been questioned by some observers.

ASEAN, CHINA, AND THE SOUTH CHINA SEA

Responding to the growing potential for conflict and the assertiveness of China's territorial claims in the SCS, the ASEAN foreign ministers adopted the ASEAN Declaration on the SCS in July 1992. The Declaration called for the peaceful resolution of "all sovereignty and jurisdictional issues pertaining to the South China Sea," the exercise of "restraint," and the application of "the principles contained in the Treaty of Amity and Cooperation in Southeast Asia as the basis for establishing a code of international conduct over the South China Sea."[7] As Emmers comments, the informal code of conduct for the SCS was based on notions of conflict management and avoidance rather than conflict resolution.[8] Despite the overlapping claims, the member states showed their interest in promoting stability in Southeast Asia and avoiding any confrontation with China. A series of informal workshops focusing on SCS disputes also began in the 1990s. As noted in the previous chapter, China began to normalize its relations with many of its neighbors. For example, China established normal diplomatic relations with Indonesia and Singapore, and in 1991, China also normalized relations with Brunei and Vietnam and was even invited that year to the ASEAN post-Ministerial Conference. An ASEAN–China dialogue was launched in 1994. Such multilateral negotiations proved successful enough to keep nonregional actors, such as the International Court of Justice (ICJ) and the UN, from any direct involvement. In fact, the five most important areas stressed in developing China-ASEAN relations cover the following aspects.[9]

1. Non-traditional security issues. This issue came to the forefront of the world community after the September 11 terrorist attack in the United States. In November 2002, the Joint Declaration of ASEAN and China on Cooperation in the Field of Non-Traditional Security Issues was adopted, which initiated full cooperation between ASEAN and China. The priorities at the current stage of cooperation include "combating trafficking in illegal drugs, people-smuggling including trafficking in women and children, sea piracy, terrorism, arms-smuggling, money-laundering, international economic crime and cyber crime."[10]

2. Free trade area arrangements. This issue marked one of the most important breakthroughs in China-ASEAN economic cooperation. The 2002 Framework Agreement on Comprehensive Economic Cooperation between ASEAN and China with the WTO rules was a milestone not only in the development of China-ASEAN comprehensive economic cooperation, but also laid the groundwork for the establishment of the China-ASEAN FTA. In East Asia, one of the most salient developments in trade regionalism is the negotiation on a free trade agreement between China and ASEAN, known as the China-ASEAN Free Trade Agreement (CAFTA).

3. In terms of bilateral and/or subregional economic development, cooperation was developing rapidly between China and ASEAN. It covers important areas of border trade between China's southwestern provinces and the newer ASEAN members; cooperation and conflict between China and riparian ASEAN countries of the Mekong River; and FDI in China and ASEAN countries. China shares land borders with several ASEAN countries and this will continue to contribute to the comprehensive development and advancement of the border regions between China and the new ASEAN members. Mekong River is regarded as the heart and soul of mainland Southeast Asia, and the upper stream of the river within the Chinese border is called Lancang River. China's hydropower projects on the Lancang River are likely to create severe environmental impact. Besides, China's competition with the ASEAN for FDI after her entry into WTO is another debate.
4. The SCS and maritime security Maritime safety could be assured through cooperation among all the interested countries in line with international law; including the 1982 UNCLOS and numerous International Maritime Organization (IMO) conventions, guidelines and directives.
5. Regional perspectives on ASEAN–China relations. The China-ASEAN FTA can have indirect but significant impact on the Korean economy. This interaction will also affect the globalization process in East Asia. Japan is taking initiatives to play a key role in peace building in areas such as Aceh and Mindanao, and in combating piracy in the Southeast Asia seas, especially the Straits of Malacca. However, Japan too feels reassured by the continuing presence of the United States as well as the balance diplomacy played by the ASEAN countries in their relations with great powers. China's fast-growing economy has become a new engine of economic growth not only for ASEAN but also for the whole East Asian region. Therefore, China has initiated the arrangement for a free trade area (FTA) agreement with ASEAN in order to avoid any disruption in China-ASEAN cooperation.

In July 1994, the ARF was created to engage the great powers and maintain regional stability. ARF emphasized institutionalization as well as norm building and capacity building, and sought to promote a collaborative security environment. The ARF, which now has 28 member states, functions as a forum that included all regional actors as members.[11] The 27th ASEAN ministerial meeting stated:

The ARF could become an effective consultative Asia-Pacific Forum for promoting open dialogue on political and security cooperation in the region. In this context, ASEAN should work with its ARF partners to bring about a more predictable and constructive pattern of relations in the Asia

Pacific.[12] The ARF's visibility as a conflict management forum increased after the resolution of the Cambodian conflict. However, outside analysts tended to be skeptical about the effectiveness of the ARF and some, such as Emmerson,[13] continue to assert that the ARF is all bark and no bite. Lim argues that the ARF gave China opportunities to divide and rule.[14] In fact, after almost 20 years, the ARF still remains at the first stage of confidence-building measures (CBMs), although its 2001 "Concept and Principles" document states that such confidence building, along with the development of preventive diplomacy and approaches to handle conflicts, is of great importance.[15]

The Council for Security Cooperation in the Asia Pacific (CSCAP)[16] also observes the ARF has not yet accomplished its mandated objectives. While the ARF has been able to undertake some CBMs, it has been reluctant or unable to advance preventive diplomacy (phase two) and conflict resolution (phase three). Unless the ARF is able to move forward in a convincing manner, there will be an opening for other options and bodies to be considered for its present role.[17] The overall picture of security cooperation in this region is thus one of flux: as new institutions are created, existing ones expand and new arrangements are formalized.[18] Acharya claims that the ARF, at the very least, still has the potential to develop norms and principles for intra-state cooperation, preventive diplomacy, and CBMs.[19] Michael Wesley argues that Asia-Pacific regionalism was always geared toward "mediating" the impacts of global order for the region.[20] In his view, after the Cold War, the ARF accommodated "the more benign aspects of world order, while keeping its more interventionist aspects at bay" by "tying the U.S. presence to the region but trying to dilute U.S. influence through diffuse and highly consensual mechanisms."[21]

China became a full Dialogue Partner of ASEAN at a July 1996 meeting in Jakarta. As discussed earlier, the five most important areas targeted for ongoing discussions were nontraditional security issues, FTA arrangements, bilateral and/or subregional economic development, the SCS and maritime security, and regional perspectives on ASEAN–China relations. China was also improving its military ties with individual ASEAN members through military training and weapons, military technology assistance, and naval port visits. Meanwhile, ASEAN–China relations had to contend with a rising China, a strong—albeit economically troubled—Japan, and, finally, the traditional superpower status of the United States. Other issues have occasionally had a spillover effect, including the cross-straits relationship between China and Taiwan, the problem of nuclear proliferation in North Korea, and the standoff between India and Pakistan in South Asia.

China was the first Nuclear Weapon State (NWS) to express its intention to accede to the Protocol to the Southeast Asia Nuclear Weapon-Free

Zone (SEANWFZ).[22] The SEANWFZ Treaty followed the provision of article VII of the 1968 Treaty on the Non-Proliferation of Nuclear Weapons, which recognizes the right of any group of states to conclude regional treaties that ensure the total absence of nuclear weapons in their respective territories. The treaty came into force in 1997 and was considered to be ASEAN's major contribution to complete elimination of nuclear weapons. Although China has indicated that it would be a signatory,[23] its deployment of ballistic missile submarines (SSBNs) to Sanya Naval Base raises serious questions about its true intentions. The relationship between ASEAN and China appeared to draw closer yet in the new millennium, with the signing of a revised Declaration on the Conduct of Parties in the SCS at an ASEAN–China summit meeting in Phnom Penh in November 2002,[24] as well as a joint declaration of the Heads of State on Strategic Partnership for Peace and Prosperity in October 2003 in Bali. Also in 2003, China signed the TAC, which enhanced the stature of that treaty as a model for interstate relations in the region. The first East Asian Summit held in Kuala Lumpur, in December 2005, involved ten ASEAN members, along with China, Japan, South Korea, India, New Zealand, and Australia, and pointedly excluded the United States. Abdul Razak Baginda commented: "There is now this feeling that we have to consult the Chinese. We have to accept some degree of Chinese leadership, particularly in light of the lack of leadership elsewhere."[25] In fact, "as long as PRC's growing eminence is perceived as beneficial for the region by key governmental elites in Southeast Asia, the international relationship between China and ASEAN will increasingly resemble hegemonic stability."[26]

In 2006, the ASEAN Defense Ministers Meeting (ADMM) were held, which envisaged the future creation of an ASEAN Security Community (ASC), and the conclusion of a formal ASEAN Charter that entered into force in December 2008. In order to meet dynamic security challenges, the Defense Ministers of ASEAN created an independent track to report directly to the ASEAN heads of state. The ASEAN Defense Ministers believed that only through constructive, open and practical cooperation among the security sectors, the region will have peace and will be able to deal with emerging security issues effectively. The objectives of ADMM Plus are to benefit ASEAN member countries in building capacity to address shared security challenges, to promote mutual trust and confidence between defense establishments through greater dialogue and transparency, to enhance regional peace and stability through cooperation in defense and security, to contribute to the realization of an ASC, and to facilitate the implementation of the Vientiane Action Program, which calls for ASEAN to build a peaceful, secure and prosperous ASEAN, and to adopt greater outward-looking external relation strategies with friends and Dialogue Partners.[27]

A 2009 meeting in Phuket, Thailand, on "Acting Together to Cope with Global Challenges,"[28] among other things, strongly reaffirmed the importance of the DOC as a milestone document between ASEAN and China to ensure peaceful resolution of disputes. In 2010, ASEAN and China also agreed to cooperate on areas such as agriculture, information and communication technology, human resource development, Mekong Basin Development, investment, energy, transport, culture, public health, tourism, and the environment.[29] Several more workshops were also conducted in 2012 in support of the DOC. These included the Workshop on Marine Hazard Prevention and Mitigation in the SCS, the Workshop on Marine Ecosystems and Biodiversity, the Symposium on Marine Ecological Environment and Monitoring Techniques, and, finally, the Joint Workshop in Commemoration of the 10th Anniversary of the DOC.

ASEAN'S POTENTIAL ROLE IN SCS DISPUTE RESOLUTION

ASEAN and China have established a significant and continuing relationship through summits, ministerial meetings, meetings between senior officials, and meetings of experts. In fact CBMs is one such method by which ASEAN has tried to resolve disputes in the SCS. In a sense, treaties like the TAC or the ASEAN Declaration of a Zone of Peace, Freedom, and Neutrality (ZOPFAN)—has not only set forth positive principles but has also been widely endorsed by all the parties, in spite of the fact that some of these treaties seriously lack implementation and enforcement mechanisms. Their aim in part is to lessen anxiety and suspicion by making the behavior of parties more predictable. Additional CBMs include regular diplomatic meetings, informal workshops, joint projects for development, scientific research, and/or environmental protection. Bilateral negotiations, mediation and/or arbitration by parties within or outside the region, and judicial settlement are obviously much more active conflict resolution measures. Since we have reviewed key treaties, declarations, and diplomatic meetings above, let us start here with workshops.

Between 1990 and 2001, a series of annual workshops were held, the first in Bali, titled workshop on managing potential conflicts in the SCS. The workshops were a direct response to Li Peng's speech in Singapore in 1990 pledging China's willingness to solve any existing conflicts peacefully.[30] The workshops convened in Indonesia were sponsored by the Canadian International Development Agency (CIDA). The participants were a mixture of both governmental and non-governmental officials, scholars, and resource people from outside the region. The objective was to provide a basis for more formal negotiations. In the end, the early workshops accomplished very little because China refused to participate, all the initiatives came from Indonesia, and ASEAN was never involved as an organization in any substantive negotiation process.[31]

Another workshop—this time, notably, outside of Indonesia—on CBMs in the SCS and Taiwan's involvement was held in 2001 in Taipei. The workshop identified a number of CBMs that might be helpful in avoiding accidental escalation of conflicts in the SCS. These included: a halt to further military construction or force buildups in disputed territories; a return to the status quo at the time of the ASEAN Declaration on the SCS; negotiations on a regionwide code of conduct to reject the use of force and to work toward the eventual demilitarization of the disputed territories; an annual environmental assessment of the SCS by private scholars; establishment of a marine park to preserve the unique biodiversity of the SCS; and joint development efforts that set aside issues of sovereignty.[32]

Another workshop was convened in Hainan in 2006 on the implementation of the Declaration on the Conduct of Parties in the SCS. In this case, the parties foresaw undertaking a few initiatives with China such as a joint ASEAN–China table top maritime search and rescue (SAR) exercise funded by the ASEAN–China Cooperation Fund (ACCF); a workshop on regional oceanographic and climate exchanges in the SCS; a workshop on disaster prevention and reduction, involving the establishment of a disaster monitoring and warning system in the SCS; and a training program on ecosystem monitoring and monitoring technology with regional oceanographic exchange around the SCS.[33] Against a backdrop of rising tensions in the SCS, a further workshop on the SCS was held in Ho Chi Minh City in 2010.[34] There was significant concern about the growing presence of naval powers in the SCS in the name of safeguarding strategic interests and counterbalancing the presence of one another. Additionally, the participants focused on the role and probable intentions of China as well as the effectiveness of the Declaration on the Conduct of Parties agreed between ASEAN and China to resolve disputes in the SCS through diplomatic means.[35]

Besides, the application of different joint development projects to resolve disputes in the SCS has been discussed for many years. In fact China has expressed its interest as well as decided to become moderately engaged in this regard. In fact, joint development is a relatively new concept in international law, dating from the 1970s. According to the British Institute of International and Comparative Law, joint development includes an agreement between two states to jointly share offshore oil and gas in a designated zone of the seabed and subsoil of the continental shelf that both or either of the participating states are entitled to under international law in proportions agreed by interstate cooperation.[36] The Institute's definition of joint development is broad enough to cover all relevant situations. The Institute specifically lists the SCS as one of the potential areas for joint development. The UNCLOS also provides a legal basis for joint development in disputed maritime areas pending the settlement of the maritime boundary delimitation. The UNCLOS leaves other options open to states concerned as to whether they can enter into joint development agreements after any definite maritime boundary delimitation. A possible Timor Gap Treaty was frequently discussed and finally accepted in 1991 in the context of possible joint development in the SCS. It suggests that instead of creating a single joint development zone, the claimants should establish 12 separate joint development zones for each area of overlapping claims.

In the 1980s, the East–West Center in Hawaii organized two workshops to discuss the possibility of joint development in the SCS. Robert Smith presented a paper at one of the workshops on potential joint development in the Spratlys. According to Smith, the claimants could draw hypothetical equidistant lines between the disputed islands and the surrounding littoral states after freezing the territorial claims.[37] Following the workshop, in 1986, Deng Xiaoping pointedly commented that the issue of the Nansha/Spratly Islands "involves more than one country."[38] He also added that from "a practical view, we opt to put aside this issue," and that "maybe in several years' time, the Chinese Government could propose a solution acceptable to all parties concerned."[39] Again, in a 1988 meeting with his Filipino counterpart, Corazon Aquino, Deng reiterated, "After many years of consideration, we think that to solve the issue [the Nansha/Spratly Islands], all parties concerned could explore joint development under the premise of admitting China's sovereignty over them."[40] However, when the Filipino government soon thereafter suggested joint use of a Chinese-built station on Mischief Reef, China demurred.

Joint development was also mentioned in the so-called "donut hole" theory proposed by Hasjim Djalal in 1989–1990. According to this theory, the zone beyond 200 miles from coastal lines and islands claimed by the concerned parties would be a zone for cooperation of all states around the SCS.[41] In 1991, the Hainan Research Institute for the SCS held a joint conference on the SCS in Hainan, at which a total of five papers dealing with joint development in the SCS were presented. The papers discussed the issue of joint development from military, economic, legal, political, and regional perspectives. Despite China's initial rebuff of the Philippines over Mischief Reef, following Deng's opening, China has been cautiously pursuing the goal of joint development in other contexts. In 2003, the China National Offshore Oil Company (CNOOC) and the Philippine National Oil Company (PNOC) agreed to jointly explore oil and gas in the SCS. China has also expressed its willingness to discuss the ways and means of joint development with other ASEAN countries, including Vietnam.

In June 2008, China and Japan reached a first-step agreement on cooperation in the East China Sea. According to Masahiko Koumura, "[T]he agreement is the first step toward realizing a common understanding between the leaders of the two countries that the East China Sea should be a Sea of Peace, Cooperation and Friendship."[42] Looking ahead, energy consumption by Asian countries is expected to increase to nearly 29.8 million barrels per day by 2025; hence, joint development should provide a remarkable window of opportunity. There are potential spinoffs as well. The joint oceanographic marine scientific expedition in the SCS is an example, where the parties have pledged to cooperate in MSR and environmental protection.[43]

Mediation, by definition, involves an invitation to presumably unbiased third parties to make nonbinding suggestions of possible terms for peaceful settlement of disputes. Some ASEAN members, especially the Philippines, have actively tried to engage the United States and Japan and even the UN as mediators, but China has consistently refused. ASEAN itself is divided over whether to engage external actors in the conflict resolution process, since this would also inevitably highlight the intra-ASEAN disputes. The resistance against involving both external states and organizations, such as UN, the ICJ and even the Asia-Pacific Economic Cooperation (APEC), is far greater than the will to engage them. For its part, China has consistently insisted that the SCS disputes must be negotiated through bilateral channels. As mentioned in the previous chapter, China has always followed "a three no's strategy" that gave China the upper hand in negotiations. This includes no internationalization of the conflict, no multilateral negotiations, and no specification of China's territorial demands.

China has also entered into bilateral negotiations when it suited China's purposes. For example, Vietnam and China held three informal meetings concerning the Cambodian conflict—in January 1989, in May 1989, and in February 1990—without any significant results. Discussions concerning the Gulf of Tonkin achieved great progress, and both parties agreed not to take any actions that would increase tensions. Moreover, bilateral negotiations between China and the Philippines have intensified since China's occupation of the Mischief Reef. There and in the Spratlys, thus far, continuing talks have at least staved off direct violent confrontations. In fact all the foregoing discussion of peaceful settlement initiatives undertaken by ASEAN has at its best simply provided a benign background of stated principles that it might have the effect of dampening the potential for conflict in the region. As noted, China resists multilateralism of existing disputes and ASEAN has its own internal divisions that constrain its members' capacity to act collectively. Southeast Asia minus ASEAN[44] would probably mean even greater political instability, more disunity, and widespread economic deterioration. That is about the best one can say for the organization. It proclaims some worthwhile principles and continues to "be there" should parties to disputes wish to make use of its services. Thus far, they have shown little inclination to do so in any particularly substantive way. Both the East Asian summits in July and November 2012 ended in dismay as Cambodia, the chair of ASEAN and an important Chinese ally, declared that the SCS disputes would not be raised in international forums. Recently, Vietnam, the Philippines, and India are all objecting to Beijing's move to establish its territorial claims by illustrating them in passports. Taiwan has also actively joined the competition by deciding to explore for undersea oil in the SCS region.

The conclusions of the ICJ with respect to the boundary cases of Pulau Ligitan and Pulau Sipadan, which was between Malaysia and Indonesia,[45] and the case of Pedra Branca/Pulau Batu Puteh, Middle Rocks, and South Ledge, which was between Malaysia and Singapore,[46] could serve as a basis for initiatives to submit the various SCS disputes to international juridical agencies like the ICJ or the International Tribunal for the Law of the Sea (ITLOS). But there are a number of complications involved. For example, matters can only be referred to the ICJ or other third-party adjudicative bodies if all parties agree. Furthermore, obviously some potential claimants are discouraged from bringing their cases to the court, because they may fear that the ruling might not be in their favor.[47] However, Philippines are an exception. They have already filed their case in front of the tribunal. In fact it is a "big and bold" move by Philippines since it is the first country to have filed a complaint against the Asian giant. Both the countries are anxiously waiting to hear back in 2016. It's a matter of time to see whether international law is able to curb or shape the desires of the Dragon. In fact on January 2016, the Philippine Supreme Court has reaffirmed the constitutionality of the 2014 Enhanced Defense Cooperation Agreement (EDCA) between the Philippines and the United States. According to the decision, the Supreme Court has paved the way for the return of forward-deployed U.S. forces to select Philippine military bases.

The ASEAN Vision 2020, which was adopted on the 30th Anniversary of ASEAN, calls for peace, stability and prosperity. Scholar's like Acharya has judged ASEAN's performance as, arguably, the world's most successful and developing regional organization.[48] The common values shared by ASEAN states are not democracy and interdependence, but rather a commitment to economic development, regime security, and political stability. These shared norms and ideas are the backbone of the constructivist analysis of Asian international relations. The ASEAN Way or, the formal management style of ASEAN, became important when the Malaysian Deputy Prime Minister Anwar Ibrahim commented that intervention is needed before simmering problems erupt into full-blown crises.[49] However, as the turmoil continues in the SCS, experts are talking about creating an ASEAN United Front, or an aggressive alliance, or even setting up a collective bargain between ASEAN and China and excluding outside powers.

It is very important to analyze how such a position might affect ASEAN. Does ASEAN need to reinvent itself and gain strategic and political prominence in order to deal with future challenges effectively? The situation looks extremely complicated since, on the one hand, ASEAN might offend China by its involvement, and on the other, if this situation continues, then general peace and prosperity will be at stake. Besides, if ASEAN unconditionally supports its members, then one or more of them might draw the organization even further into the conflict. Although differences still exist between ASEAN and China, Rosenberg remarks that both have established a promising strategic partnership to ensure peace and cooperation for the region.[50] What is required right now is to predict new challenges that will continue to emerge and test the strength of this partnership as well as the possible trajectories of ASEAN–China relations based on such challenges.

With regard to the relative success of various forms and modes of security cooperation in the Asia-Pacific region, the motivation of actors engaged in such cooperative security efforts requires more consideration. There are combinations of liberal institutionalist and constructivist explanations that begin from the premise that benefits are accrued in terms of cost reduction when a group of states agrees to ensure transparency, coordination, and regulation. With growing regional interdependence and an increase in transnational issues, the need for conscious coordination of policies with neighbors deepens. This may lead to a sense of regional identity and community and make the use of force in security matters unlikely.[51] In fact, these approaches help to explain the formation of ASEAN and other organizations. Growing competition between claimants as well as non-claimant states and an increased power position of some states have together complicated the situation in this region. Moreover, in the wake of the post-2008 financial crisis, a conceptual linkage has developed between economic and strategic security, which is especially noticeable in the case of ASEAN plus THREE (APT), the Boao Forum, and Asian Cooperation Dialogue. Hence what might be envisaged now is a more independent concept of "strategic economic security" with clear economic imperative.[52]

The question might arise as to why severe military conflict has not broken out between the ASEAN countries. Well the reason might be the consistent adherence to the principle of non-interference by the ASEAN countries. In this case, constructivism can be understood as a positive social process that can have a transforming impact on the relationships among ASEAN countries. Constructivism makes the assumption that the interests of states and identities are endogenous, which means that institutions can provide a place for states to develop a sense of a shared identity and purpose. The concept of security communities is particularly helpful in terms of shaping an understanding of the importance of such communities in the region. The end of the Cold War, the resurgence of China, the Asian economic crisis, and the events of September 11th have all contributed to such changes in the Asia-Pacific security architecture. In fact all these are intertwined with an increase in multilateral efforts including the ARF, APEC, and the Shangri-La dialogue and also the success of some modes of security cooperation over others.[53]

The two main factors that have so far prevented these hot spots from deteriorating into a major crisis are mutual deterrence and a focus on goals that would be damaged were war to break out. The question arises whether ASEAN really matter in regional security? For the realists and neorealists, the answer might be no. However, for neoliberals and social constructivists, the answer is that ASEAN helps to create a common identity and social norms conducive to regional stability. Although the organization continues to have major weaknesses and limitations, ASEAN matters since it enhances the efficiency of state cooperation. In 2015 ASEAN was scheduled to become a full-fledged community consisting of political-security, economics, and societal-human rights. Of course, how far that vision will become successful remains to be seen in the future. Although ASEAN's integration continues to be problematic and its ability to speak in a unified fashion about politico-security matters remains uncertain, a strong ASEAN still appears to be desired by most of the SCS claimants. Be that as it may, a number of scholars who profoundly disagree with the norms of non-interference and call for its revision are nonetheless convinced of its continuing capacity to bind the conduct of ASEAN member states. Despite minor differences in interpretation, the ASEAN way is regarded as a series of behavioral and procedural norms shared by ASEAN member countries in practicing diplomacy. The ASEAN Way would serve as a mechanism for conflict prevention and China's involvement with ASEAN may help to curb the risk of violence. ASEAN has been pushing hard to call for tangible resolutions to end the SCS dispute. In this case one of the most comprehensive one is ASEAN's six-point principles on the SCS.[54] According to this principle, the member states would look for the following:

a. The full implementation of the Declaration on the Conduct of Parties in the SCS (2002);
b. The Guidelines for the Implementation of the Declaration on the Conduct of Parties in the SCS (2011);
c. The early conclusion of a Regional Code of Conduct in the SCS;

d. The full respect of the universally recognized principles of International Law, including the 1982 UNCLOS;
e. The continued exercise of self-restraint and nonuse of force by all parties; and
f. The peaceful resolution of disputes, in accordance with universally recognized principles of International Law, including the 1982 UNCLOS.

Despite potential challenges, there is hope that China and ASEAN will resolve their differences over the SCS dispute. In fact some of the multilateral proposals such as the 2014 cooperation proposals from ASEAN states for the second round of competition for projects for the cooperation fund; the Code for Unplanned Encounters at Sea (CUES), or the 2015 ASEAN–China Year of Maritime Cooperation and so on. would not only create favorable conditions for better maritime cooperation but would also shape a new pattern of diplomatic relations with neighboring countries. Besides, the Sunnylands summit[55] that was hosted in 2016 by the U.S. president Barack Obama in Rancho Mirage, California, laid the groundwork for the current and future place of Southeast Asia and ASEAN in the U.S. foreign policy. The summit was an opportunity to make positive progress on advancing the U.S.-ASEAN strategic partnership on the one hand (be it the Trans-Pacific Partnership or the SCS dispute) and proposing a concrete plan of action to be implemented by 2020 on the other. Nonetheless, for ASEAN, the summit was an occasion to demonstrate its importance in handling regional and global challenges.

Finally, the last chapter will summarize the findings of the study and suggest few lines of possible future research that might prove fruitful for policymakers and/or academics.

NOTES

1. "The Founding of ASEAN," The Official Website of ASEAN, http://www.aseansec.org/20024.htm.
2. Ibid.
3. Ibid.
4. "Overview of ASEAN," The Official Website of ASEAN.
5. Ibid.
6. Amitav Acharya, *Constructing a Security Community in Southeast Asia: ASEAN and the Problem of Regional Order* (New York: Routledge, 2009): 5–6; On October 23, 1991, the Agreements on a Comprehensive Political Settlement of the Cambodia Conflict were signed by Cambodia and 18 other nations in the presence of the United Nations and ASEAN. The agreements were the culmination of more than a decade of negotiations in which the Secretary-General had been closely involved from the outset.

7. "ASEAN Declaration on The South China Sea, Manila, Philippines, July 22, 1992," Association of Southeast Asian Nations web site, http://www.aseansec.org/3634.htm, accessed March 10, 2013.

8. Emmers Ralf, "The Changing power distribution in the South China Sea: Implications for Conflict Management and Avoidance," RSIS Working Paper, no. 183, (September 30, 2009).

9. John, Wong, et al. "New Dimensions in China-ASEAN Relations," in China-ASEAN relations: Economic and legal dimensions, ed. Wong (Hackensack, NJ: World Scientific Publishing Company, 2006).

10. See Joint Declaration of ASEAN and China on Cooperation in the Field of Non-Traditional Security Issues, Sixth ASEAN-China Summit, Phnom Penh, Cambodia, November 4, 2002, http://www.aseansec.org/13185.htm.

11. These include Australia, Bangladesh, Brunei Darussalam, Cambodia, Canada, China, European Union, India, Indonesia, Japan, Democratic Peoples' Republic of Korea, Republic of Korea, Laos, Malaysia, Myanmar, Mongolia, New Zealand, Pakistan, Papua New Guinea, Philippines, Russian Federation, Singapore, Sri Lanka, Thailand, Timor Leste, the United States, and Vietnam.

12. Chheang Vannarith, "Asia Pacific Security Issues: Challenges and Adaptive Mechanism," *Cambodian Institute for Cooperation and Peace Policy Brief* 3 (July 2010).

13. Ibid.

14. Ibid.

15. ASEAN Secretariat (2001), ASEAN Regional Forum (ARF): Concept and Principles of Preventive Diplomacy, http://www.aseansec.org/3571.htm, accessed December 13, 2010.

16. The Council for Security Cooperation in the Asia-Pacific is a non-governmental process for dialogue on security issues in Asia Pacific. There are currently twenty member committees of CSCAP.

17. Chheang Vannarith, "Asia Pacific Security Issues: Challenges and Adaptive Mechanism," 2010.

18. Evelyn Goh and Amitav Acharya, "Introduction: Reassessing Security Cooperation in the Asia-Pacific," in *Reassessing Security Cooperation in the Asia-Pacific Competition, Congruence, and Transformation*, ed. Amitav Acharya and Evelyn Goh (Cambridge, MA: MIT Press, 2007).

19. Amitav Acharya, "Preventive Diplomacy: Issues and Institutions in the Asia Pacific Region," Paper Presented to the Eighth Asia-Pacific Roundtable, Kuala Lumpur, (June 6–8, 1994).

20. Michael Wesley, "Meditating the Global Order: The Past and Future of Asia-Pacific Regional Organizations," in *Asia Pacific Security: Policy Challenges*, ed. David Lovell (Singapore: ISEAS, 2003), 161.

21. Ibid.

22. SEANWFZ is a nuclear weapons moratorium treaty conducted between ten Southeast Asian members in 1995 under the auspices of the ASEAN. It is also known as the Bangkok treaty.

23. Carlyle Thayer, "Recent Developments in the South China Sea: Implications for Peace, Stability and Cooperation in the Region," Paper presented on "The South

China Sea: Cooperation for Regional Security and Development," co-organized by Diplomatic Academy of Vietnam and the Vietnam Lawyers' Association Hanoi, Socialist Republic of Vietnam (November, 2009).

24. Amitav Acharya, Constructing a Security Community in Southeast Asia, 6.

25. Edward Cody, "China's Quiet Rise Casts Wide Shadow," *Washington Post*, 2005.

26. Jorn Dosch, "Managing Security in ASEAN-China Relations: Liberal Peace of Hegemonic Stability," *Asian Perspective* 31, no.1 (2007): 209-236.

27. Cheang Vannarith, "Asia Pacific Security Issues: Challenges and Adaptive Mechanism," *Cambodian Institute for Cooperation and Peace Policy Brief* 3, July 2010.

28. The Official Website of ASEAN: visit http://www.aseansec.org/, http://www.asean.org/communities/asean-political-security-community/item/joint-communique-of-the-42nd-asean-foreign-ministers-meeting-acting-together-to-cope-with-global-challenges-phuket-thailand-20-july-2009.

29. Ibid.

30. The Official Website of ASEAN: visit http://www.aseansec.org/, http://www.asean.org/news/asean-secretariat-news/item/initiatives-on-south-china-sea-conflict-resolution-and-peacekeeping-cooperation-people-engagement-among-many-issues-noted-in-comprehensive-asean-joint-communique.

31. The Official Website of ASEAN: visit http://www.aseansec.org/, [accessed March 10, 2013], http://www.asean.org/asean/external-relations/china/item/asean-china-dialogue-relations.

32. Yann-Huei Song, "The Overall Situation in the South China Sea in the New Millennium: Before and After the September 11 Terrorist Attacks," *Ocean Development and International Law*, 2003.

33. Nguyen Thao and Ramses Amer, "A New Legal Arrangement for the South China Sea?" *Ocean Development and International Law*, 2009.

34. 2nd International Workshops on the South China Sea: Cooperation for Regional Security and Development, Ho Chi Minh City, November 11–12, 2011, Maritime Institute of Malaysia.

35. Ibid.

36. Ibid.

37. Robert W. Smith, "Joint (Development) Zones: A Review of Past Practice and Thoughts on the Future" in *Sustainable Development and Preservation of the Oceans: The Challenges of UNCLOS and Agenda 21*, eds. Mochtar Kusuma-Atmadja, Thomas A. Mensah and Bernard H. Oxman (Honolulu, the Law of the Sea Institute, University of Hawaii, 1997), 661.

38. Schofield Clive, "Maritime energy resources in Asia: Legal Regimes and Cooperation," *The National Bureau of Asian Research*, no. 37 (February 2012): 94.

39. Ibid.

40. Ibid.

41. Nguyen Thao and Ramses Amer, "A New Legal Arrangement for the South China Sea?" *Ocean Development and International Law* 40, no. 333 (2009): 349.

42. Ibid.

43. Henry S. Bensurto, "Cooperation in the South China Sea: Views on the Philippines—Vietnam Cooperation on Maritime and Ocean Concerns," South China Sea Studies (July, 2011): "Maritime Energy Resources in Asia, Legal Regimes and Cooperation," NBR Special Report no. 37 (February, 2012).

44. The Official Website of ASEAN: visit http://www.aseansec.org/,http://www.asean.org/asean/about-asean/history/item/the-future-of-asean, accessed March 10, 2013.

45. Case Concerning Sovereignty over Pulau Ligitan and Pulau Sipadan (Indonesia/Malaysia), Judgment of 17 December 2002, available at the Web site of the International Court of Justice at www.icj-cij.org/docket/files/102/7714.pdf.

46. Case Concerning Sovereignty over Pedra Branca/Pulau Batu Puteh, Middle Rocks and South Ledge (Malaysia/Singapore), Judgment of 23 May 2008, available at the Web site of the International Court of Justice at www.icj-cij.org/docket/files/130/14492.pdf.

47. Nguyen Thao and Ramses Amer, "A New Legal Arrangement for the South China Sea?" *Ocean Development and International Law*, 2009.

48. Amitya Acharya, *Constructing a Security Community in Southeast Asia: ASEAN and the Problem of Regional Order* (New York: Routledge Publications, 2000).

49. Ibrahim Anwar, "Crisis Prevention," *Newsweek International*, July 21, 1997, 13.

50. David Rosenberg, Review of ASEAN-China Relations: Realities and Prospects, ed. Saw Swee-Hock, Sheng Lijun and Chin Kin Wah, *The China Journal* 56 (July 2006), http://community.middlebury.edu/~scs/docs/Rosenberg,%20David.ASEAN-China%20Relations- Review.pdf.

51. Robert Gilpin, *The Political Economy of International Relations* (Princeton, NJ: Princeton University Press, 1987).

52. Helen Nesadurai, *Globalization and Economic Security in East Asia* (London: Routledge, 2005).

53. Amitav Acharya, "Regional Institutions and Security in the Asia Pacific: Evolution, Adaptation and Prospects for Transformation," *Reassessing Security Cooperation in the Asia-Pacific: Competition, Congruence, and Transformation* (Cambridge, MA: The MIT Press, 2007).

54. Prasanth Parameswaran, "Why the US-ASEAN Sunnylands Summit Matters," *The Diplomat*, February 11, 2016. http://thediplomat.com/2016/02/why-the-us-asean-sunnylands-summit-matters/.

55. Ibid.

Chapter 6

The Road to Peace

What an endgame might look like? Well, the world expects a grand solution to the SCS dispute, but it looks like that this will be a long time in coming. In fact a sudden major military outbreak could not be ruled out entirely in the SCS. However, the author agrees with Noordin's remark, that it is always good to make peace while there is peace. In fact there is no right or wrong time for this.[1] What it means for the SCS dispute is that while tension gets reduced for whatever reasons, cooperative commitments and functional arrangements should be negotiated not only for the interest of the claimants but also for China as well. Unfortunately the road to peace is not easy and appears to be unlikely within the foreseeable future.

The book addresses the most important question as to what factors have increased the probability of conflicts in the SCS? As explained earlier, the SCS holds major resource reserves of a variety of minerals and fish that are certain to be exploited (perhaps overexploited) in future years, especially with rapidly improving technology. This region is also the locus of some of the most strategic and busiest shipping lanes in the world, the importance of which are likely to increase dramatically in future years. Regrettably for the cause of peace, the SCS is additionally the site of numerous islands and other less substantial territorial outcroppings, some which have long been in dispute and others in more recent times. Historical titles and claims have often been as vague as many of the documents and maps upon which they have been based. Although the UNCLOS as an international legal regime has clarified some of the rules affecting maritime traffic and territorial disputes in the SCS, but paradoxically did add to the competition by codifying such concepts as 12-mile territorial waters and 200-mile EEZ.

China's new assertiveness in the SCS region has raised tensions and high-lighted the need for all potential claimants to make or reaffirm their claims, clarify their extent, and prepare to defend them, militarily if necessary. The disputes have the potential of escalating into serious international conflicts, not only because of the practical resource stakes, but also because emotions run high whenever the themes of challenges to sovereignty and national pride are sounded. In IR theory terms, there are thus strong realist incentives for conflict as well as constructivist dimensions, insofar as the numerous parties to disputes assess the strength and significance of their own claims and degree of commitment to them, as well as the elusive "actual" intentions of their rivals. In fact, the long-range threat from China may yet prove to be far less serious than some analysts and policy-makers suppose. However much depends on the priority China attaches to expansionism in the SCS, when the country has so many other regional concerns (political, military, security, economic)—Taiwan, North Korea, Japan, and of course not to mention problems at home. Yes, China's economic progress has been striking, but Beijing still has a host of political, economic, and social problems to overcome. Some observers say that China's aging authoritarian regime may ultimately be unable to cope with the major challenges that lie ahead. Whether domestic instability would lead to more or less saber rattling in the SCS is extremely hard to predict.

The United States has recently announced that it would shift the bulk of its naval fleet including as many as six aircraft carriers to the Pacific Ocean by 2020, China commented that it is "advisable for some to refrain from muddying the waters and fishing the rein and for some others to desist from dancing behind a Pied Piper whose magic tone, as tempting as it is, might lead its followers astray."[2] China insisted that the much-hyped Chinese threat to the freedom of navigation in the SCS is purely imaginary. China has already seen its political, economic, and military strength grow markedly; hence, according to Chinese authorities, fabricating new claims is not in the nation's agenda. Rather, Beijing genuinely wishes to turn the SCS into a sea of peace, friendship, and cooperation. In China's view, the United States is making a steady and deliberate effort to bolster the U.S. role in the region. For example, the United States has refused for quite some time to sign the UNCLOS, partly because some have feared that the provisions will limit the free navigational rights of U.S. warships in the EEZs of other countries. But now China believes that any U.S. decision to join the convention would be a signal of it's growing intentions to get involved in SCS disputes.

Regarding the contributions of ASEAN in managing conflicts in the SCS region, I think that perhaps ASEAN has mainly acted as a candidate who is always being present as an organization. ASEAN has continually attempted to establish and reiterate a central norm of interstate relations for the region: that Southeast Asia is a zone of cooperation and peace, where states have firmly pledged to resolve any and all disputes peacefully. Accordingly, direct condemnation of any member or external party is not helpful and, given the regional norm, should hardly ever be required. In IR theory terms, this "ASEAN way" is pure "social construction," but it has some significant "objective reality," because it has been supported by the likes of countless declarations, meetings, and workshops and at least has dependably in a positive and upbeat tone discouraged conflict rather than make it more likely. Nonetheless, the question remains whether such a benign approach is not itself marginal to the realpolitik that appears to characterize the SCS ambitions of a rising China and other regional claimants, not to mention the concerns of external powers like the United States and India. The proof will most likely be in the pudding in the years ahead. Will the parties—not least China—embrace and explore the full potential of the ASEAN way or prove the ASEAN way to have been, at best, well-intentioned moralizing or, at worst, gravely deficient because it failed to fashion an urgently needed more activist approach to conflict resolution?

Finally, what is the likely utility of other conflict prevention mechanisms in the SCS region? Probably I should have phrased this as "other means of preventing conflict" and made the question less distinct from the one regarding ASEAN, because that organization has pointed to the potential usefulness of such measures (beyond ASEAN itself) as joint development projects and resource sharing. In fact, we have noted that China has been willing to "dialogue" on a formal basis with ASEAN but has consistently rejected any true multilateralization of SCS disputes. Moreover, as we have observed, ASEAN has pridefully resisted calling upon external powers or organizations like the UN to exercise their good offices, mediate, or arbitrate disputes in the region. Parties to territorial claims appear to be more anxious to keep their future options open, rather than risk closing them off prematurely through any compromise settlement. This may reflect the perceived domestic utility of persistent foreign frictions and/or a genuine belief that it is too early to know what strategic and resource rewards might eventually prove to be at stake. Nevertheless, this book makes a few modest suggestions for various potential "win-win" measures that might help to advance cooperation and lower tensions in future years.

A FEW CONSTRUCTIVE SUGGESTIONS

In sum, I personally think that the SCS disputes are very likely to remain much as they currently are for quite some time, with minor skirmishes in the region frequently making front-page news. While actions and counteractions by other claimants with regard to their claims over the islands in the SCS are to be expected, I believe that such actions will probably not escalate to a grave conflict that would threaten the entire region. However, admittedly, the situation is extremely volatile and could indeed give rise to warfare beyond the level of a skirmish and even involve active military engagement by external powers like the United States. Given that very real possibility, it obviously behooves all parties concerned to explore any and all possible win-win solutions and, following the ASEAN way, to continue to stress cooperation over confrontation at every possible opportunity.

One positive approach is expanding economic interdependence and joint development projects. As we know from the classic example of World War I, for example, there is no guarantee that close economic ties will prevent the outbreak of war. But, all other things being equal, enmeshing parties in a mutually beneficial web of economic interdependence certainly cannot hurt the prospects for peace. It is significant that after the 2008 financial crisis, a conceptual linkage has apparently begun to develop between economic and strategic security. This is particularly noticeable in the case of APT and the Asian Cooperation Dialogue.[3] Members should develop a common ASEAN vision for future East Asian trade and economic integration, perhaps looking to create an ASEAN-wide FTA and a full-fledged ASEAN economic community by 2020. It is a generally healthy trend that ASEAN–China economic relations have been growing rapidly over the past decade. China is currently the second largest trading partner of ASEAN, and ASEAN is the third largest trading partner of China. Further intra-ASEAN economic integration and also with China could help counterbalance the new trans-Pacific free trade agreement now being pursued by the United States.

Due to the increase in the number and intensity of regional maritime security problems in the SCS, it is high time for the states to initiate an effective and stable management regime. Cooperation between and among SCS claimants should be encouraged to set up regimes for the effective use of natural resources, perhaps starting with the management of fishery resources, with the hope of having a spillover effect on other areas of collaboration. Due to increased pressure on both living and nonliving resources, there is a need for strategies to cooperatively manage fishing, shipping traffic, and the environment in the SCS region. The parties should actively investigate successful agreements for joint fishing management zones, protection of diminishing coral reefs, and hydrocarbon exploration, as well as more general nature conservation zones, especially those administered by independent or multilateral agencies. There might also be joint efforts to expand tourism in the region, with an emphasis on "eco-tourism."

Military-to-military consultation and collaboration is also urgently needed to minimize the threat of dangerous incidents that could escalate to full-fledged armed conflict. Countries might lower tensions by expanding agreement on military rules of engagement and offering prior notification of the nature and intention of military movements/exercises in the SCS. In my view, joint patrols and even joint access to commercially available satellite and other information showing developments on disputed features should be promoted in order to respond to illegal fishing and to enhance antipiracy efforts as well as the safety and freedom of navigation generally. Monitoring and documenting military deployments and unauthorized civilian landings by nationalist groups could be useful to all concerned. Regular sharing of information using the Geographic Information System or the GIS technology (another upcoming and significant research area) should be given precedence in order to avoid possible miscalculations at sea.

Another area for potential cooperation is that of SAR operations. With regard to the International Convention on Maritime Search and Rescue,[4] the IMO found that China is mainly responsible for whatever SAR work already exists in the SCS region. In order to strengthen its SAR capability, China will have to build airports and ports, which would no doubt be seen as threatening by other SCS parties. Thus, more equitable burden sharing of SAR might be beneficial from more than one standpoint.

This book has gathered together and analyzed a wide range of information on the evolving SCS disputes, much of it new to the limited major literature on this subject, partly because events in the region have been moving so rapidly in recent years. As the situation continues to evolve in future years, there will certainly be no shortage of opportunities for additional research. For example, I had briefly mentioned China's Arctic strategy in the previous chapter. Because of China's quest for natural resources, China will continue to make its presence felt in the Arctic and, minimally, look to the Arctic for potential imports of resources. The question remains whether China will opt for the notion of an Arctic open to all, and what will be the effect of its Arctic strategy on the intensity of its bargaining claims in the SCS?

Last but not the least, a word on IR theory and the SCS disputes. Mine was never intended to be a book focusing on IR theory, rather—like all the other major works in the literature on this subject (except for Acharya's constructivist view of ASEAN)—mainly a forthright review and analysis of ongoing territorial disputes in the SCS, their possible escalation, and avenues for advancing cooperation rather than conflict. However, to be sure, the SCS disputes inevitably have theoretical overtones. China's pursuit of its perceived "core interests," as well as other parties' defense of theirs,' is clearly realist. China's rise calls to mind neorealism's concern with global structure and power shifts. China's engagement with a wide variety of international organizations from the UN to the WTO to ASEAN points to liberal institutionalism. And the concept of the ASEAN way as well as the various SCS parties' different conceptions of their own claims and the threat posed by others belongs to the constructivists. Thus, although I have not cast my book primarily in a theoretical mode, the challenge to do so remains for those bold enough to attempt it. I wish them well.

NOTES

1. Valencia Mark, "Whither the South China Sea Disputes?" *South China Sea Studies* (July 2010).
2. Times of India, "China Warns US from 'Muddying Waters' in South China Sea," June 3, 2012, http://articles.timesofindia.indiatimes.com/2012-06-03/china/32005634_1_south-china-sea-naval-fleetchina-claims.
3. ASEAN Plus Three is a forum that functions as a coordinator of cooperation between ASEAN and three East Asian countries like Japan, China, and South Korea. It is credited for creating the financial stability in Asia. The Asia Cooperation Dialogue is a body created in 2002 to promote Asian cooperation at a continental level and to help integrate separate regional cooperation organizations. The first leaders meeting were held in 1996 and 1997.
4. China's Search and Rescue Efforts in South China Sea Seriously Lacking. 2013. *Global Times* (March 18, 2013).

Appendix 1

The 2002 ASEAN–China Declaration on the Conduct of the Parties in the South China Sea

The Governments of the Member States of ASEAN and the Government of the People's Republic of China,

REAFFIRMING their determination to consolidate and develop the friendship and cooperation existing between their people and governments with the view to promoting a twenty-first century-oriented partnership of good neighborliness and mutual trust;

COGNIZANT of the need to promote a peaceful, friendly and harmonious environment in the South China Sea between ASEAN and China for the enhancement of peace, stability, economic growth and prosperity in the region;

COMMITTED to enhancing the principles and objectives of the 1997 Joint Statement of the Meeting of the Heads of State/Government of the Member States of ASEAN and President of the People's Republic of China;

DESIRING to enhance favourable conditions for a peaceful and durable solution of differences and disputes among countries concerned;

HEREBY DECLARE the following:

1. The Parties reaffirm their commitment to the purposes and principles of the Charter of the United Nations, the 1982 UN Convention on the Law of the Sea, the Treaty of Amity and Cooperation in Southeast Asia, the Five Principles of Peaceful Coexistence, and other universally recognized principles of international law which shall serve as the basic norms governing state-to-state relations;

2. The Parties are committed to exploring ways for building trust and confidence in accordance with the above-mentioned principles and on the basis of equality and mutual respect;

3. The Parties reaffirm their respect for and commitment to the freedom of navigation in and overflight above the South China Sea as provided for by the universally recognized principles of international law, including the 1982 UN Convention on the Law of the Sea;

4. The Parties concerned undertake to resolve their territorial and jurisdictional disputes by peaceful means, without resorting to the threat or use of force, through friendly consultations and negotiations by sovereign states directly concerned, in accordance with universally recognized principles of international law, including the 1982 UN Convention on the Law of the Sea;

5. The Parties undertake to exercise self-restraint in the conduct of activities that would complicate or escalate disputes and affect peace and stability including, among others, refraining from action of inhabiting on the presently uninhabited islands, reefs, shoals, cays, and other features and to handle their differences in a constructive manner.
   Pending the peaceful settlement of territorial and jurisdictional disputes, the Parties concerned undertake to intensify efforts to seek ways, in the spirit of cooperation and understanding, to build trust and confidence between and among them, including:
   a. holding dialogues and exchange of views as appropriate between their defense and military officials; b. ensuring just and humane treatment of all persons who are either in danger or in distress;
   c. notifying, on a voluntary basis, other Parties concerned of any impending joint/combined military exercise; and d. exchanging, on a voluntary basis, relevant information.

6. Pending a comprehensive and durable settlement of the disputes, the Parties concerned may explore or undertake cooperative activities. These may include the following:
   a. marine environmental protection; b. marine scientific research; c. safety of navigation and communication at sea; d. search and rescue operation; and e. combating transnational crime, including but not limited to trafficking in illicit drugs, piracy and armed robbery at sea, and illegal traffic in arms.
   The modalities, scope and locations, in respect of bilateral and multilateral cooperation should be agreed upon by the Parties concerned prior to their actual implementation.

7. The Parties concerned stand ready to continue their consultations and dialogues concerning relevant issues, through modalities to be agreed by them, including regular consultations on the observance of this

Declaration, for the purpose of promoting good neighbourliness and transparency, establishing harmony, mutual understanding and cooperation, and facilitating peaceful resolution of disputes among them;

8. The Parties undertake to respect the provisions of this Declaration and take actions consistent therewith;
9. The Parties encourage other countries to respect the principles contained in this Declaration;
10. The Parties concerned reaffirm that the adoption of a code of conduct in the South China Sea would further promote peace and stability in the region and agree to work, on the basis of consensus, towards the eventual attainment of this objective.

Done on the Fourth Day of November in the Year Two Thousand and Two in Phnom Penh, the Kingdom of Cambodia.

Appendix 2

EEZ Rules under Part V of UNCLOS

ARTICLE 55

Specific legal regime of the exclusive economic zone

The exclusive economic zone is an area beyond and adjacent to the territorial sea, subject to the specific legal regime established in this Part, under which the rights and jurisdiction of the coastal State and the rights and freedoms of other States are governed by the relevant provisions of this Convention.

ARTICLE 56

Rights, jurisdiction and duties of the coastal State in the exclusive economic zone

1. In the exclusive economic zone, the coastal State has:
   (a) sovereign rights for the purpose of exploring and exploiting, conserving and managing the natural resources, whether living or non-living, of the waters superjacent to the seabed and of the seabed and its subsoil, and with regard to other activities for the economic exploitation and exploration of the zone, such as the production of energy from the water, currents and winds;
   (b) jurisdiction as provided for in the relevant provisions of this Convention with regard to:
      (i) the establishment and use of artificial islands, installations and structures;
      (ii) marine scientific research;
      (iii) the protection and preservation of the marine environment;
   (c) other rights and duties provided for in this Convention.

2. In exercising its rights and performing its duties under this Convention in the exclusive economic zone, the coastal State shall have due regard to the rights and duties of other States and shall act in a manner compatible with the provisions of this Convention.
3. The rights set out in this article with respect to the seabed and subsoil shall be exercised in accordance with Part VI.

ARTICLE 57

Breadth of the exclusive economic zone

The exclusive economic zone shall not extend beyond 200 nautical miles from the baselines from which the breadth of the territorial sea is measured.

ARTICLE 58

Rights and duties of other States in the exclusive economic zone

1. In the exclusive economic zone, all States, whether coastal or land-locked, enjoy, subject to the relevant provisions of this Convention, the freedoms referred to in article 87 of navigation and overflight and of the laying of submarine cables and pipelines, and other internationally lawful uses of the sea related to these freedoms, such as those associated with the operation of ships, aircraft and submarine cables and pipelines, and compatible with the other provisions of this Convention.
2. Articles 88 to 115 and other pertinent rules of international law apply to the exclusive economic zone in so far as they are not incompatible with this Part.
3. In exercising their rights and performing their duties under this Convention in the exclusive economic zone, States shall have due regard to the rights and duties of the coastal State and shall comply with the laws and regulations adopted by the coastal State in accordance with the provisions of this Convention and other rules of international law in so far as they are not incompatible with this Part.

ARTICLE 59

Basis for the resolution of conflicts regarding the attribution of rights and jurisdiction in the exclusive economic zone

In cases where this Convention does not attribute rights or jurisdiction to the coastal State or to other States within the exclusive economic zone, and a conflict arises between the interests of the coastal State and any other State or States, the conflict should be resolved on the basis of equity and in the light of all the relevant circumstances, taking into account the respective importance of the interests involved to the parties as well as to the international community as a whole.

ARTICLE 60

Artificial islands, installations and structures in the exclusive economic zone

1. In the exclusive economic zone, the coastal State shall have the exclusive right to construct and to authorize and regulate the construction, operation and use of:
   (a) artificial islands;
   (b) installations and structures for the purposes provided for in article 56 and other economic purposes;
   (c) installations and structures which may interfere with the exercise of the rights of the coastal State in the zone.
2. The coastal State shall have exclusive jurisdiction over such artificial islands, installations and structures, including jurisdiction with regard to customs, fiscal, health, safety and immigration laws and regulations.
3. Due notice must be given of the construction of such artificial islands, installations or structures, and permanent means for giving warning of their presence must be maintained. Any installations or structures which are abandoned or disused shall be removed to ensure safety of navigation, taking into account any generally accepted international standards established in this regard by the competent international organization. Such removal shall also have due regard to fishing, the protection of the marine environment and the rights and duties of other States. Appropriate publicity shall be given to the depth, position and dimensions of any installations or structures not entirely removed.
4. The coastal State may, where necessary, establish reasonable safety zones around such artificial islands, installations and structures in which it may take appropriate measures to ensure the safety both of navigation and of the artificial islands, installations and structures.
5. The breadth of the safety zones shall be determined by the coastal State, taking into account applicable international standards. Such zones shall be designed to ensure that they are reasonably related to the nature and function of the artificial islands, installations or structures, and shall not exceed a distance of 500 metres around them, measured from each point of

their outer edge, except as authorized by generally accepted international standards or as recommended by the competent international organization. Due notice shall be given of the extent of safety zones.

6. All ships must respect these safety zones and shall comply with generally accepted international standards regarding navigation in the vicinity of artificial islands, installations, structures and safety zones.

7. Artificial islands, installations and structures and the safety zones around them may not be established where interference may be caused to the use of recognized sea lanes essential to international navigation.

8. Artificial islands, installations and structures do not possess the status of islands. They have no territorial sea of their own, and their presence does not affect the delimitation of the territorial sea, the exclusive economic zone or the continental shelf.

ARTICLE 61

Conservation of the living resources

1. The coastal State shall determine the allowable catch of the living resources in its exclusive economic zone.

2. The coastal State, taking into account the best scientific evidence available to it, shall ensure through proper conservation and management measures that the maintenance of the living resources in the exclusive economic zone is not endangered by over-exploitation. As appropriate, the coastal State and competent international organizations, whether sub regional, regional or global, shall cooperate to this end.

3. Such measures shall also be designed to maintain or restore populations of harvested species at levels which can produce the maximum sustainable yield, as qualified by relevant environmental and economic factors, including the economic needs of coastal fishing communities and the special requirements of developing States, and taking into account fishing patterns, the interdependence of stocks and any generally recommended international minimum standards, whether sub regional, regional or global.

4. In taking such measures the coastal State shall take into consideration the effects on species associated with or dependent upon harvested species with a view to maintaining or restoring populations of such associated or dependent species above levels at which their reproduction may become seriously threatened.

5. Available scientific information, catch and fishing effort statistics, and other data relevant to the conservation of fish stocks shall be contributed and exchanged on a regular basis through competent international

organizations, whether sub regional, regional or global, where appropriate and with participation by all States concerned, including States whose nationals are allowed to fish in the exclusive economic zone.

ARTICLE 62

Utilization of the living resources

1. The coastal State shall promote the objective of optimum utilization of the living resources in the exclusive economic zone without prejudice to article 61.
2. The coastal State shall determine its capacity to harvest the living resources of the exclusive economic zone. Where the coastal State does not have the capacity to harvest the entire allowable catch, it shall, through agreements or other arrangements and pursuant to the terms, conditions, laws and regulations referred to in paragraph 4, give other States access to the surplus of the allowable catch, having particular regard to the provisions of articles 69 and 70, especially in relation to the developing States mentioned therein.
3. In giving access to other States to its exclusive economic zone under this article, the coastal State shall take into account all relevant factors, including, inter alia, the significance of the living resources of the area to the economy of the coastal State concerned and its other national interests, the provisions of articles 69 and 70, the requirements of developing States in the sub region or region in harvesting part of the surplus and the need to minimize economic dislocation in States whose nationals have habitually fished in the zone or which have made substantial efforts in research and identification of stocks.
4. Nationals of other States fishing in the exclusive economic zone shall comply with the conservation measures and with the other terms and conditions established in the laws and regulations of the coastal State. These laws and regulations shall be consistent with this Convention and may relate, inter alia, to the following:
   (a) licensing of fishermen, fishing vessels and equipment, including payment of fees and other forms of remuneration, which, in the case of developing coastal States, may consist of adequate compensation in the field of financing, equipment and technology relating to the fishing industry;
   (b) determining the species which may be caught, and fixing quotas of catch, whether in relation to particular stocks or groups of stocks or catch per vessel over a period of time or to the catch by nationals of any State during a specified period;

    (c) regulating seasons and areas of fishing, the types, sizes and amount of gear, and the types, sizes and number of fishing vessels that may be used;

    (d) fixing the age and size of fish and other species that may be caught;

    (e) specifying information required of fishing vessels, including catch and effort statistics and vessel position reports;

    (f) requiring, under the authorization and control of the coastal State, the conduct of specified fisheries research programs and regulating the conduct of such research, including the sampling of catches, disposition of samples and reporting of associated scientific data;

    (g) the placing of observers or trainees on board such vessels by the coastal State;

    (h) the landing of all or any part of the catch by such vessels in the ports of the coastal State;

    (i) terms and conditions relating to joint ventures or other cooperative arrangements;

    (j) requirements for the training of personnel and the transfer of fisheries technology, including enhancement of the coastal State's capability of undertaking fisheries research;

    (k) enforcement procedures.

5. Coastal States shall give due notice of conservation and management laws and regulations.

ARTICLE 63

Stocks occurring within the exclusive economic zones of two or more coastal States or both within the exclusive economic zone and in an area beyond and adjacent to it

1. Where the same stock or stocks of associated species occur within the exclusive economic zones of two or more coastal States, these States shall seek, either directly or through appropriate sub regional or regional organizations, to agree upon the measures necessary to coordinate and ensure the conservation and development of such stocks without prejudice to the other provisions of this Part.

2. Where the same stock or stocks of associated species occur both within the exclusive economic zone and in an area beyond and adjacent to the zone, the coastal State and the States fishing for such stocks in the adjacent area shall seek, either directly or through appropriate sub regional or regional organizations, to agree upon the measures necessary for the conservation of these stocks in the adjacent area.

ARTICLE 64

Highly migratory species

1. The coastal State and other States whose nationals fish in the region for the highly migratory species listed in Annex I shall cooperate directly or through appropriate international organizations with a view to ensuring conservation and promoting the objective of optimum utilization of such species throughout the region, both within and beyond the exclusive economic zone. In regions for which no appropriate international organization exists, the coastal State and other States whose nationals harvest these species in the region shall cooperate to establish such an organization and participate in its work.
2. The provisions of paragraph 1 apply in addition to the other provisions of this Part.

ARTICLE 65

Marine mammals

Nothing in this Part restricts the right of a coastal State or the competence of an international organization, as appropriate, to prohibit, limit or regulate the exploitation of marine mammals more strictly than provided for in this Part. States shall cooperate with a view to the conservation of marine mammals and in the case of cetaceans shall in particular work through the appropriate international organizations for their conservation, management and study.

ARTICLE 66

Anadromous stocks

1. States in whose rivers anadromous stocks originate shall have the primary interest in and responsibility for such stocks.
2. The State of origin of anadromous stocks shall ensure their conservation by the establishment of appropriate regulatory measures for fishing in all waters landward of the outer limits of its exclusive economic zone and for fishing provided for in paragraph 3(b). The State of origin may, after consultations with the other States referred to in paragraphs 3 and 4 fishing these stocks, establish total allowable catches for stocks originating in its rivers.
3. (a) Fisheries for anadromous stocks shall be conducted only in waters landward of the outer limits of exclusive economic zones, except in cases

where this provision would result in economic dislocation for a State other than the State of origin. With respect to such fishing beyond the outer limits of the exclusive economic zone, States concerned shall maintain consultations with a view to achieving agreement on terms and conditions of such fishing giving due regard to the conservation requirements and the needs of the State of origin in respect of these stocks.

    (b) The State of origin shall cooperate in minimizing economic dislocation in such other States fishing these stocks, taking into account the normal catch and the mode of operations of such States, and all the areas in which such fishing has occurred.

    (c) States referred to in subparagraph (b), participating by agreement with the State of origin in measures to renew anadromous stocks, particularly by expenditures for that purpose, shall be given special consideration by the State of origin in the harvesting of stocks originating in its rivers.

    (d) Enforcement of regulations regarding anadromous stocks beyond the exclusive economic zone shall be by agreement between the State of origin and the other States concerned.

4. In cases where anadromous stocks migrate into or through the waters landward of the outer limits of the exclusive economic zone of a State other than the State of origin, such State shall cooperate with the State of origin with regard to the conservation and management of such stocks.

5. The State of origin of anadromous stocks and other States fishing these stocks shall make arrangements for the implementation of the provisions of this article, where appropriate, through regional organizations.

ARTICLE 67

Catadromous species

1. A coastal State in whose waters catadromous species spend the greater part of their life cycle shall have responsibility for the management of these species and shall ensure the ingress and egress of migrating fish.

2. Harvesting of catadromous species shall be conducted only in waters landward of the outer limits of exclusive economic zones. When conducted in exclusive economic zones, harvesting shall be subject to this article and the other provisions of this Convention concerning fishing in these zones.

3. In cases where catadromous fish migrate through the exclusive economic zone of another State, whether as juvenile or maturing fish, the management, including harvesting, of such fish shall be regulated by agreement between the State mentioned in paragraph 1 and the other State concerned.

Such agreement shall ensure the rational management of the species and take into account the responsibilities of the State mentioned in paragraph 1 for the maintenance of these species.

ARTICLE 68

Sedentary species

This Part does not apply to sedentary species as defined in article 77, paragraph 4.

ARTICLE 69

Right of land-locked States

1. Land-locked States shall have the right to participate, on an equitable basis, in the exploitation of an appropriate part of the surplus of the living resources of the exclusive economic zones of coastal States of the same sub region or region, taking into account the relevant economic and geographical circumstances of all the States concerned and in conformity with the provisions of this article and of articles 61 and 62.
2. The terms and modalities of such participation shall be established by the States concerned through bilateral, sub regional or regional agreements taking into account, inter alia:
   (a) the need to avoid effects detrimental to fishing communities or fishing industries of the coastal State;
   (b) the extent to which the land-locked State, in accordance with the provisions of this article, is participating or is entitled to participate under existing bilateral, sub regional or regional agreements in the exploitation of living resources of the exclusive economic zones of other coastal States;
   (c) the extent to which other land-locked States and geographically disadvantaged States are participating in the exploitation of the living resources of the exclusive economic zone of the coastal State and the consequent need to avoid a particular burden for any single coastal State or a part of it;
   (d) the nutritional needs of the populations of the respective States.
3. When the harvesting capacity of a coastal State approaches a point which would enable it to harvest the entire allowable catch of the living resources in its exclusive economic zone, the coastal State and other States concerned shall cooperate in the establishment of equitable arrangements

on a bilateral, sub regional or regional basis to allow for participation of developing land-locked States of the same sub region or region in the exploitation of the living resources of the exclusive economic zones of coastal States of the sub region or region, as may be appropriate in the circumstances and on terms satisfactory to all parties. In the implementation of this provision the factors mentioned in paragraph 2 shall also be taken into account.

4. Developed land-locked States shall, under the provisions of this article, be entitled to participate in the exploitation of living resources only in the exclusive economic zones of developed coastal States of the same sub region or region having regard to the extent to which the coastal State, in giving access to other States to the living resources of its exclusive economic zone, has taken into account the need to minimize detrimental effects on fishing communities and economic dislocation in States whose nationals have habitually fished in the zone.

5. The above provisions are without prejudice to arrangements agreed upon in sub regions or regions where the coastal States may grant to land-locked States of the same sub region or region equal or preferential rights for the exploitation of the living resources in the exclusive economic zones.

ARTICLE 70

Right of geographically disadvantaged States

1. Geographically disadvantaged States shall have the right to participate, on an equitable basis, in the exploitation of an appropriate part of the surplus of the living resources of the exclusive economic zones of coastal States of the same sub region or region, taking into account the relevant economic and geographical circumstances of all the States concerned and in conformity with the provisions of this article and of articles 61 and 62.

2. For the purposes of this Part, "geographically disadvantaged States" means coastal States, including States bordering enclosed or semi-enclosed seas, whose geographical situation makes them dependent upon the exploitation of the living resources of the exclusive economic zones of other States in the sub region or region for adequate supplies of fish for the nutritional purposes of their populations or parts thereof, and coastal States which can claim no exclusive economic zones of their own.

3. The terms and modalities of such participation shall be established by the States concerned through bilateral, sub regional or regional agreements taking into account, inter alia:

   (a) the need to avoid effects detrimental to fishing communities or fishing industries of the coastal State;

(b) the extent to which the geographically disadvantaged State, in accordance with the provisions of this article, is participating or is entitled to participate under existing bilateral, sub regional or regional agreements in the exploitation of living resources of the exclusive economic zones of other coastal States;

(c) the extent to which other geographically disadvantaged States and land-locked States are participating in the exploitation of the living resources of the exclusive economic zone of the coastal State and the consequent need to avoid a particular burden for any single coastal State or a part of it;

(d) the nutritional needs of the populations of the respective States.

4. When the harvesting capacity of a coastal State approaches a point which would enable it to harvest the entire allowable catch of the living resources in its exclusive economic zone, the coastal State and other States concerned shall cooperate in the establishment of equitable arrangements on a bilateral, sub regional or regional basis to allow for participation of developing geographically disadvantaged States of the same sub region or region in the exploitation of the living resources of the exclusive economic zones of coastal States of the sub region or region, as may be appropriate in the circumstances and on terms satisfactory to all parties. In the implementation of this provision the factors mentioned in paragraph 3 shall also be taken into account.

5. Developed geographically disadvantaged States shall, under the provisions of this article, be entitled to participate in the exploitation of living resources only in the exclusive economic zones of developed coastal States of the same sub region or region having regard to the extent to which the coastal State, in giving access to other States to the living resources of its exclusive economic zone, has taken into account the need to minimize detrimental effects on fishing communities and economic dislocation in States whose nationals have habitually fished in the zone.

6. The above provisions are without prejudice to arrangements agreed upon in sub regions or regions where the coastal States may grant to geographically disadvantaged States of the same sub region or region equal or preferential rights for the exploitation of the living resources in the exclusive economic zones.

ARTICLE 71

Non-applicability of articles 69 and 70

The provisions of articles 69 and 70 do not apply in the case of a coastal State whose economy is overwhelmingly dependent on the exploitation of the living resources of its exclusive economic zone.

ARTICLE 72

Restrictions on transfer of rights

1. Rights provided under articles 69 and 70 to exploit living resources shall not be directly or indirectly transferred to third States or their nationals by lease or license, by establishing joint ventures or in any other manner which has the effect of such transfer unless otherwise agreed by the States concerned.
2. The foregoing provision does not preclude the States concerned from obtaining technical or financial assistance from third States or international organizations in order to facilitate the exercise of the rights pursuant to articles 69 and 70, provided that it does not have the effect referred to in paragraph 1.

ARTICLE 73

Enforcement of laws and regulations of the coastal State

1. The coastal State may, in the exercise of its sovereign rights to explore, exploit, conserve and manage the living resources in the exclusive economic zone, take such measures, including boarding, inspection, arrest and judicial proceedings, as may be necessary to ensure compliance with the laws and regulations adopted by it in conformity with this Convention.
2. Arrested vessels and their crews shall be promptly released upon the posting of reasonable bond or other security.
3. Coastal State penalties for violations of fisheries laws and regulations in the exclusive economic zone may not include imprisonment, in the absence of agreements to the contrary by the States concerned, or any other form of corporal punishment.
4. In cases of arrest or detention of foreign vessels the coastal State shall promptly notify the flag State, through appropriate channels, of the action taken and of any penalties subsequently imposed.

ARTICLE 74

Delimitation of the exclusive economic zone between States with opposite or adjacent coasts

1. The delimitation of the exclusive economic zone between States with opposite or adjacent coasts shall be effected by agreement on the basis of

international law, as referred to in Article 38 of the Statute of the International Court of Justice, in order to achieve an equitable solution.

2. If no agreement can be reached within a reasonable period of time, the States concerned shall resort to the procedures provided for in Part XV.

3. Pending agreement as provided for in paragraph 1, the States concerned, in a spirit of understanding and cooperation, shall make every effort to enter into provisional arrangements of a practical nature and, during this transitional period, not to jeopardize or hamper the reaching of the final agreement. Such arrangements shall be without prejudice to the final delimitation.

4. Where there is an agreement in force between the States concerned, questions relating to the delimitation of the exclusive economic zone shall be determined in accordance with the provisions of that agreement.

ARTICLE 75

Charts and lists of geographical coordinates

1. Subject to this Part, the outer limit lines of the exclusive economic zone and the lines of delimitation drawn in accordance with article 74 shall be shown on charts of a scale or scales adequate for ascertaining their position. Where appropriate, lists of geographical coordinates of points, specifying the geodetic datum, may be substituted for such outer limit lines or lines of delimitation.

2. The coastal State shall give due publicity to such charts or lists of geographical coordinates and shall deposit a copy of each such chart or list with the Secretary-General of the United Nations.

Appendix 3

Summary of the 2002 ASEAN Declaration on the South China Sea

WE, the foreign Ministers of the member countries of the Association of Southeast Asian Nations; RECALLING the historic, cultural and social ties that bind our peoples as states adjacent to the South China Sea;

WISHING to promote the spirit of kinship, friendship and harmony among our peoples who share similar Asian traditions and heritage;

DESIROUS of further promoting conditions essential to greater economic cooperation and growth; RECOGNIZING that we are bound by similar ideals of mutual respect, freedom, sovereignty and jurisdiction of the parties directly concerned;

RECOGNIZING that South China Sea issues involve sensitive questions of sovereignty and jurisdiction of the parties directly concerned;

CONSCIOUS that any adverse developments in the South China Sea Directly affect peace and stability in the region.

HEREBY EMPHASIZE the necessity to resolve all sovereignty and jurisdictional issues pertaining to the South China Sea by peaceful means, without resort to force;

URGE all parties concerned to exercise restraint with view to creating a positive climate for the eventual resolution of all disputes;

RESOLVE, without prejudicing the sovereignty and jurisdiction of countries having direct interests in the area, to explore the possibility cooperation in the South China Sea relating to the safety of maritime navigation and communication, protection against pollution of the marine environment, coordination of search and rescue operations, efforts towards combating piracy and armed robbery as well as collaboration in the campaign against illicit trafficking in drugs;

COMMEND all parties concerned to apply the principles contained in the Treaty of Amity and Cooperation in Southeast Asia as the basis for establishing a code of international conduct over the South China Sea;

INVITE all parties concerned to subscribe to this Declaration of principles. Signed in Manila, Philippines, this 22nd day of July, nineteen hundred and ninety-two.

Bibliography

2nd International Workshop on the South China Sea: Cooperation for Regional Security and Development, Ho Chi Minh City, November 11–12, 2011, Maritime Institute of Malaysia.

Acharya, Amitav. "Preventive Diplomacy: Issues and Institutions in the Asia Pacific Region," Paper Presented to the Eighth Asia-Pacific Roundtable, June, 1994.

———. *Constructing a Security Community in Southeast Asia: ASEAN and the Problem of Regional Order*. New York: Routledge Publications, 2009.

———. *Seeking Security In The Dragon's Shadow: China and Southeast Asia In The Emerging Asian Order*. Singapore: Institute of Defence and Strategic Studies, March 2003.

———. "Regional Institutions and Security in the Asia Pacific: Evolution, Adaptation and Prospects for Transformation." In *Reassessing Security Cooperation in the Asia-Pacific: Competition, Congruence, and Transformation*, edited by Amitav Acharya and Evelyn Goh, 19–40. Cambridge, Massachusetts: MIT Press, 2007.

———. "East Asia's Arrested Regionalism." Paper presented at the Asian Studies Seminar, St Antony's College, Oxford, February 23, 2007.

———."Can Asia Step Up to 21st Century Leadership?" Yale Global, December 1, 2011. http://yaleglobal.yale.edu/content/can-asia-step-21st-century-leadership.

Akpan, Rita. "China, the Spratly Islands Territorial Dispute and Multilateral Cooperation- An Exercise in Realist Rhetoric or Mere Diplomatic Posturing? A Critical Review." Center for Energy, Petroleum and Mineral Law and Policy, University of Dundee, Scotland, February 2003. http://www.dundee.ac.uk/cepmlp/gateway/index.php?news=27994.

Alatas, H. E. Mr. Ali. Opening Address at the first workshop on "Managing Potential Conflicts in the South China Sea," Denpasar, Bali, January 22, 1990.

Ang Cheng, Guan. "ASEAN, China and the South China Sea Dispute." *Security Dialogue* 30, no. 4 (1999): 425–30.

Anwar, Ibrahim. "Crisis Prevention." *Newsweek International*, July 21, 1997.

Asian Wall Street Journal. "Asia Slips into Irrelevance." November 5, 2002.

Asia Times. "India Challenges China in South China Sea." April 26, 2000. http://www/atimes.com/ind-pak/BD27Df01.html.

Association of Southeast Nations (ASEAN). "Opening Statement By H.E. Professor S. Jayakumar Minister for Foreign Affairs of Singapore." ASEAN Ministerial Meeting, Subang Jaya, Malaysia, May 24, 1997.

———. ASEAN Declaration on the South China Sea. July 22, 1992. http://www.aseansec.org/1545.htm.

———. "The ASEAN Troika. Terms of Reference Adopted at the 33rd AMM," July 24–25, 2000, Bangkok. http://www.aseansec.org/3637.htm.

———. "ASEAN Regional Forum (ARF): Concept And Principles of Preventive Diplomacy," Adopted at the 8th RAF, July 25, 2001. http://www.aseansec.org/3571.htm.

———. "Joint Declaration of ASEAN and China on Cooperation in the Field of Non-Traditional Security Issues." Sixth ASEAN–China Summit, Phnom Penh, Cambodia, November 4, 2002. http://www.aseansec.org/13185.htm.

———. The Official Website of ASEAN. http://www.aseansec.org/.

Association of Southeast Nations Secretariat. ASEAN Regional Forum: Concept and Principles of Preventive Diplomacy. 2001. http://www.aseansec.org/3571.htm.

Baker, John C., and David G. Wiencek, eds. *Cooperative Monitoring in the South China Sea: Satellite Imagery, Confidence-Building Measures, and the Spratly Islands Disputes*. London: Praeger, 2002.

Bateman, Sam."UNCLOS and Its Limitations as the Foundation for a Regional Maritime Regime." Working Paper No. 111, Institute of Defense and Strategic Studies, Singapore, 2006.

———. "The Regime of the South China Sea – The Significance of the Declaration on the Conduct of Parties." https://blog.canpan.info/oprf/img/858/dr.bateman_presentation.pdf.

Bautista, Lowell B. "Thinking Outside the Box: The South China Sea Issue and the United Nations Convention on the Law of the Sea (Options, Limitations and Prospects)." *Philippines Law Journal* 81 (2006): 699–731.

———. "Maritime Energy Resources in Asia, Legal Regimes and Cooperation." *National Bureau of Asian Research*. Special Report no. 37 (February 2012).

Baviera, Aileen S. P. "Territorial disputes in East Asia: Proxies for China-US strategic competition?" *East Asia Forum*, November 27, 2010. http://www.eastasiaforum.org/2010/11/27/territorial-disputes-in-east-asia-proxies-for-china-us-strategic-competition/.

BBC News China. "China morning round up: China-Japan islands dispute." July 12, 2012.

BBC News Asia. "South China Sea tension tops Asean regional agenda." July 9, 2012.

———. "South China Sea: Beijing attacks US trouble-making." August 6, 2012.

———. "South Korea's Lee Myung-bak visits disputed islands." August 10, 2012.

Beckman, Robert. "The China–Philippines dispute in the South China Sea: Does Beijing have a legitimate claim?" *East Asia Forum*, March 28, 2012. http://www.eastasiaforum.org/2012/03/28/the-china-philippines-dispute-in-the-south-china-sea-does-beijing-have-a-legitimate-claim/.

_____. "South China Sea: Worsening Dispute or Growing Clarity in Claims." RSIS Commentaries, August 16, 2010. http://www.rsis.edu.sg/publications/Perspective/RSIS0902010.pdf.

Bennett, Michael. "The People's Republic of China and the use of International Law in the Spratly Island Dispute." *Stanford Journal of International Law* 28 (Spring 1992): 425–50.

Bensurto, Henry S. "Cooperation in the South China Sea: Views on the Philippines—Vietnam Cooperation on Maritime and Ocean Concerns." Paper presented at the South China Sea Studies Second International Workshop, Ho Chi Minh City, Vietnam, November 2010. http://nghiencuubiendong.vn/en/conferences-and-seminars-/second-international-workshop/593-593.

Bercovitch, Jacob, Victor Kremenyuk, and I. William Zartman, eds. *The SAGE Handbook of Conflict Resolution Problem-Solving Approaches.* Thousand Oaks, CA: Sage, 2009.

Blunden, Margaret. "Geopolitics and the Northern Sea Route." *International Affairs* 88, no. 1 (2012): 115–129.

Bradford, John. "The Growing Prospects for Maritime Security Cooperation in Southeast Asia." *Naval War College Review* 58, no. 3 (2005): 63–86.

Brago, Pia Lee. "China says 4 patrol ships in West Phl Sea back in Guangzhou." *Philippine Star*, July 7, 2012, http://www.philstar.com/headlines/2012/07/10/826275/china-says-4-patrol-ships-west-phl-sea-back-guangzhou.

_____. "China Insists on Bilateral Talks on Spratlys." *Philippine Star*, September 28, 2011. http://www.philstar.com/headlines/731660/china-insists-on-bilateral-talks-on-spratlys.

Bumiller, Elisabeth."U.S. to Sustain Military Power in the Pacific." *New York Times*, October 23, 2011. http://www.nytimes.com/2011/10/24/world/asia/panetta-tells-pacific-countries-that-us-will-keep-strong-presence.html?_r=0.

Buszynski, Leszek. "Rising Tensions in the South China Sea: Prospects for a Resolution of the Issue." *Security Challenges* 6, no. 2 (2010): 85–104.

Buszynski, Leszek and Iskandar Sazlan. "Maritime Claims and Energy Cooperation in the South China Sea." *Contemporary Southeast Asia* 29, no. 1 (2007): 143–71.

Calder, Kent E. "China and Japan's Simmering Rivalry." *Foreign Affairs* 85, no. 2 (2006): 129–39.

Campbell, Caitlin. "China and the Arctic: Objectives and Obstacles." U.S.-China Economic and Security Review Commission Staff Research Report, 2012. http://www.uscc.gov/researchpapers/2012/China-and-the-Arctic_Apr2012.pdf.

Catley, Bob and Makmur Keliat. *Spratlys: The Dispute in the SCS.* Singapore: Ashgate, 1997.

Chakraborti, Tridib. "The Territorial Claims in South China Sea: Probing Persistent Uncertainties." In *Peoples Republic of China at Fifty: Politics, Economy and Foreign Relations*, edited by Arun Kumar Banerji and Purusottam Bhattacharya, 171–207. New Delhi: Lancer Publication, 2001.

Chan, John. "US-China tensions over South China Sea." World Socialist Web Site. August 4, 2010. http://www.wsws.org/en/articles/2010/08/usch-a04.html.

Chanda, Nayan. "South China Sea: Treacherous Shoals." *Far Eastern Economic Review* 155, no. 32 (August 13, 1992): 14–17.

Chen, Sulan. *Instrumental and Induced Cooperation: Environmental Politics in the South China Sea*. College Park, MD: University of Maryland, 2005.

Chengxin, Pan. "Is the South China Sea a new 'Dangerous Ground' for US-China rivalry?" *East Asia Forum*, May 24, 2011. http://www.eastasiaforum.org/2011/05/24/is-the-south-china-sea-a-new-dangerous-ground-for-us-china-rivalry/.

Cheung, Tai Ming. "The Balance Tilts." *Far Eastern Economic Review*141, no. 39 (September 29, 1988): 40–1.

Chin, Chin Yoon. "Potential For Conflict in the Spratly Islands." Master's thesis, Naval Postgraduate School, Monterey, CA, 2003.

China Post. "Report Claims Chinese Airstrip Near Disputed Islands Near Completion." May 27, 2012.

Ching, Frank. "East Asia's Free for All- Territorial disputes with South Korea and China over islets reveal rising nationalism, Japan's weakness." Yale Global, August 30, 2012. http://yaleglobal.yale.edu/content/east-asias-free-all.

Clinton, Hillary Rodham. Remarks at Press Availability. National Convention Center, Hanoi, Vietnam, July 23, 2010. http://www.state.gov/secretary/rm/2010/07/145095.htm.

Cody, Edward. "China's Quiet Rise Casts Wide Shadow." *Washington Post*, February 26, 2005. http://www.washingtonpost.com/wp-dyn/articles/A54610-2005Feb25.html.

Cossa, Ralph, ed. "Confidence Building Measures in the South China Sea." *Pacific Forum* SIS, No. 2-01 (August 2001).

Coulter, Daniel. "South China Sea Fisheries: Countdown to Calamity." *Contemporary Southeast Asia* 17, no. 4 (March 1996): 371–88.

Cronin, Richard P. "Maritime Territorial Disputes and Sovereignty Issues in Asia." Testimony before the Senate Subcommittee on East Asia and Pacific Affairs, July 15, 2009.

Dasgupta, Saibal. "Vietnamese Threat to China, from the Sea?" *Times of India*, June 12, 2011. http://articles.timesofindia.indiatimes.com/2011-06-12/china/29649924_1_south-china-sea-chinese-fishermen-ammunition-drill.

Deccan Herald. "China Questions US Interest in Signing UN Convention on Seas." May 26, 2012. http://www.deccanherald.com/content/252352/china-questions-us-interest-signing.html.

Devonshire-Ellis, Chris. "China's String of Pearls Strategy." *China Briefing*, March 18, 2009. http://www.china-briefing.com/news/2009/03/18/china%E2%80%99s-string-of-pearls-strategy.html.

Dosch, Jorn. "Managing Security in ASEAN-China Relations: Liberal Peace of Hegemonic Stability." *Asian Perspective* 31, no. 1 (2007): 209–36.

Dutton, Peter. "Three Disputes and Three Objectives: China and the South China Sea." *Naval War College Review* 64, no. 4 (2011): 42–67.

Dzurek, Daniel, "China Occupies Mischief Reef in Latest Spratly Gambit." *IBRU Boundary and Security Bulletin* 3, no. 1 (April 1995): 65–71.

———. "The Spratly Islands Dispute: Who's On First?" *International Boundaries Research Unit Maritime Briefing* 2, no. 1. Durham, UK: IBRU, 1996.

Economist. "China's Assertiveness at Sea- Choppy Waters East and South, China Makes a Splash." January 21, 2010. http://www.economist.com/node/15331153.

Economic Times. "South China Sea an Area of 'Significant Concern': Indian Navy Chief." *The Economic Times*, November 17, 2011. http://articles. economictimes.indiatimes.com/2011-11-17/news/30410113_1_south-china-sea-indian-navy-territorial-disputes.

Emmers, Ralf. "The Influence of the Balance of Power Factor within the ASEAN Regional Forum." *Contemporary Southeast Asia* 23, no. 2 (2001): 275–91.

———."Maritime Disputes in the South China Sea: Strategic and Diplomatic Status Quo." Working Paper No. 87, Institute of Defence and Strategic Studies, Singapore, 2005. http://www.rsis.edu.sg/publications/WorkingPapers/WP87. pdf.

———. "Introduction: The South China Sea: Towards a Cooperative Management Regime." In *Security and International Politics in the South China Sea: Towards a Co-operative Management Regime*, edited by Sam Bateman and Ralf Emmers, 1–4. London: Routledge, 2009.

———. "The Changing power distribution in the South China Sea: Implications for Conflict Management and Avoidance." RSIS Working Paper, no. 183 (September 2009).

Emmerson, Donald K. "What Do the Blind-Sided See? Reapproaching Regionalism in Southeast Asia." *The Pacific Review* 18, no. 1 (2005): 1–21.

Esplanada, Jerry. "China not pulling out 7 vessels around Scarborough Shoal." *Philippine Daily Inquirer,* June 19, 2012.

Fackler, Martin. "Under Diplomatic Strain, Japan Recalls Envoy in Dispute With China Over Islands." *New York Times*, July 15, 2012.

Foot, Rosemary. "Modes of Regional Conflict Management: Comparing Security Cooperation in the Korean Peninsula, China-Taiwan, and the South China Sea." In *Reassessing Security Cooperation in the Asia-Pacific Competition, Congruence, and Transformation*, edited by Amitav Acharya and Evelyn Goh, 93–112. Cambridge, MA: MIT Press, 2007.

Friedman, Thomas. "Containment-Lite." *New York Times*, November 9, 2010. http:// www.nytimes.com/2010/11/10/opinion/10friedman.html.

Friedberg, Aaron. "China's Challenge at Sea." *New York Times*, September 4, 2011. http://www.nytimes.com/2011/09/05/opinion/chinas-challenge-at-sea.html.

Garnaut, John. "China Warns on US-Australian Ties." *The Age*, June 7, 2012. http:// www.theage.com.au/national/china-warns-on-usaustralian-ties-20120606-1zwp0. html.

Garver, John. "China's Push Through the South China Sea: The Interactions of Bureaucratic and National Interests." *The China Quarterly* 132 (December 1992): 999–1028.

Gault, Ian Townsend. "Legal and Political Perspectives On Sovereignty Over The Spratly Islands." Paper presented at the Workshop on the South China Sea Conflict Organized by the Center for Development and Environment, University of Oslo, Oslo, April 24–26, 1999.

George, Alexander and Andrew Bennett. *Case Studies and Theory Development in the Social Sciences*. Cambridge, MA: MIT Press, 2005.

Gertz, Bill. "China Builds Up Strategic Sea Lanes." *Washington Times*, January 17, 2005. http://www.washingtontimes.com/news/2005/jan/17/20050117-115550-1929r/.

Gilpin, Robert. *The Political Economy of International Relations*. Princeton, NJ: Princeton University Press, 1987.

Gjetnes, Marius. "The Legal Regime of Islands in The South China Sea." Master's thesis, University of Oslo, Norway, 2000.

Glaser, Bonnie, and Evan Medeiros. "The Changing Ecology of Foreign Policy-Making in China: The Ascension and Demise of the Theory of 'Peaceful Rise'." *China Quarterly* 190 (2007): 291–310.

Global Times. "Don't Take Peaceful Approach for Granted." October 25, 2011. http://www.globaltimes.cn/.

———."China opposes application of U.S.-Japan security treaty to Diaoyu Islands." August 26, 2012. http://www.globaltimes.cn/content/729056.shtml.

———."China's Search and Rescue Efforts in South China Sea Seriously Lacking." March 18, 2013. http://www.globaltimes.cn/.

GMA News Online. "China to Build Communication Network Covering South China Sea Islets." September 14, 2012. http://www.gmanetwork.com/news/story/273945/news/world/china-to-build-communication-network-covering-south-china-sea-islets.

Grant, Jeremy, Ben Bland and Gwen Robinson. "South China Sea Issue Divides ASEAN." FT. COM, July 16, 2012. http://www.ft.com/cms/s/0/3d45667c-cf29-11e1-bfd9-00144feabdc0.html#axzz2JwWktyU9.

Haacke, Jurgen. *ASEAN's Diplomatic and Security Culture: Origins, Development and Prospects*. London: Routledge, 2003.

Haller-Trost, R. "International Law and the History of the Claims to the Spratly Islands 10." Paper presented at the South China Sea Conference, American Enterprise Institute, September 7–9, 1994.

Hancox, David and Victor Prescott. "A Geographical Description of the Spratly Islands and an Account of Hydrographic Surveys among those Islands." *IBRU* 1, no. 6 (1995).

Hartcher, Peter. "US Finds Unwilling Partner in China to Avert Potential Crisis in Region." *Sydney Morning Herald*, August 17, 2011. http://www.smh.com.au/world/us-finds-unwilling-partner-in-china-to-avert-potential-crisis-in-region-20110816-1iwge.html.

Harris, Stuart and Mack Andrew, eds. *Asia-Pacific Security: The Economics-Politics Nexus*. New South Wales: Allen and Unwin, 1997.

Hasjim, Djalal. 2001. "Indonesia and the SCS Initiative." *Ocean Development and International Law* 32, no. 2 (2001): 97–105.

Hawksley, Humphrey and Simon Holberton. *Dragonstrike: The Milennium War*. New York: St. Martin's Press, 1997.

Herberg, Mikkel, E. "Asia's Energy Insecurity: Cooperation or Conflict?" In *Strategic Asia 2004–05: Confronting Terrorism in the Pursuit of Power*, edited by A. J. Tellis and M. Wills, 339–77. Seattle: The National Bureau of Asian Research, 2005.

———. "Natural Gas in Asia: History and Prospects." *The National Bureau of Asian Research*, Pacific Energy Summit, 2011.

Hille, Kathrin. "Clinton Struggles to Soothe Beijing Fears." *The Financial Times*, September 5, 2012. http://www.ft.com/cms/s/0/9b296eec-f728-11e1-8e9e-00144feabdc0.html.

Hiramatsu, Shigeo. "Chinas Advances in the South China Sea: Strategies and Objectives." *Asia-Pacific Review* 8, no.1 (2001): 40–50.

Holland, Lisa. "China Celebrates Its Growing Military Might." Yahoonews.com. August 1, 2012. http://uk.news.yahoo.com/china-celebrates-growing-military-might-074525669.html.

Holmes, James R. "South China Sea Is No Black Sea." *The Diplomat,* October 5, 2011. http://thediplomat.com/2011/10/05/south-china-sea-is-no-black-sea/.

Hong, Nong. "Chinese Perceptions of the SCS Dispute." *Geopolitics of Energy* 30, no. 6 (June 2008).

———. "The Melting Arctic and Its Impact on China's Maritime Transport." *Research in Transportation Economics* 35, no. 1 (May 2012): 50–7.

———. *UCLOS and Ocean Dispute Settlement: Law and Politics in the South China Sea.* New York: Routledge, 2012.

———. "Face-Off in the South China Sea: Conflict or Compromise?" Asia Maritime Transparency Initiative, March 2015.

http://amti.csis.org/the-post-reclamation-scenario-in-the-south-china-sea-the-role-of-china-and-the-united-states/.

Hopf, Ted. "The Promise of Constructivism in International Relations Theory." *International Security* 23, no. 1 (1998): 171–200.

Hutchison, Jason. "The South China Sea: Confusion in Complexity." *Critique: A Worldwide Student Journal of Politics* (Spring 2004): 103–25.

Hyer, Eric. "The South China Sea Disputes: Implications of China's Earlier Territorial Settlements." *Pacific Affairs* 68, no. 1 (1995): 34–54.

Information Office of the State Council of the People's Republic of China. "China's National Defense in 2008." January 2009.

International Court of Justice. Case Concerning Sovereignty over Pulau Ligitan and Pulau Sipadan (Indonesia/Malaysia), Judgment of 17 December 2002, www.icj-cij.org/docket/files/102/7714.pdf.

———. Case Concerning Sovereignty over Pedra Branca/Pulau Batu Puteh, Middle Rocks and South Ledge (Malaysia/Singapore), Judgment of 23 May 2008. www.icj-cij.org/docket/files/130/14492.pdf.

Jacobs, Andrew. "China Warns U.S. to Stay Out of Islands Dispute." *New York Times,* July 26, 2010. http://www.nytimes.com/2010/07/27/world/asia/27china.html.

Jacobs, Bruce. "China's frail historical claims to the South China and East China Seas." American Enterprise Institute, June 26, 2014. https://www.aei.org/publication/chinas-frail-historical-claims-to-the-south-china-and-east-china-seas/.

Ji, Guoxing. *The Spratly Disputes and Prospects for Settlement.* Kuala Lumpur, Malaysia: Institute of Strategic and International Studies, 1992.

Jinming, Li and Li Dexia. "The Dotted Line on the Chinese Map of the South China Sea: A Note." *Ocean Development and International Law* 34 (2003): 287–95.

Joint Declaration of ASEAN and China on Cooperation in the Field of Non-Traditional Security Issues. Sixth ASEAN-China Summit, Phnom Penh, Cambodia, November 4, 2002. http://www.aseansec.org/13185.htm.

Joyner, Christopher. "The Spratly Islands Dispute in the South China Sea: Problems, Policies, and Prospects for Diplomatic Accommodation." In *Investigating*

Confidence Building Measures in the Asia Pacific Region Report 28, edited by Ranjeet Singh. Washington, DC: Henry L. Stimson Center, 1999.

———. "The Spratly Islands Dispute: Legal Issues and Prospects for Diplomatic Accommodation." In *Cooperative Monitoring in the South China Sea: Satellite Imagery, Confidence Building Measures, and the Spratly Island Disputes*, edited by John Baker and David Wiencek. Westport, CT: Praeger, 2002.

Kang, David C. "U.S. Alliances and the Security Dilemma in the Asia-Pacific." In *Reassessing Security Cooperation in the Asia-Pacific Competition, Congruence, and Transformation*, edited by Amitav Acahrya and Evelyn Goh, 71–92. Cambridge, MA: MIT Press, 2007.

Kaplan, Robert. "The South China Sea Is the Future of Conflict." *Foreign Policy Issue* 188 (October 2011): 1–8.

Karagiannis, Emmanuel. "China's Pipeline Diplomacy: Assessing the Threat of Low-Intensity Conflicts." *Harvard Asia Quarterly* (Winter 2010): 54–60.

Kastner, Jens. "Taiwan circling South China Sea bait." *Asia Times Online*, June 12, 2012. http://centurychina.com/plaboard/posts/3907063.shtml.

———. "Beijing Exhibiting New Assertiveness in South China Sea." *The New York Times*, May 31, 2012. http://www.nytimes.com/2012/06/01/world/asia/beijing-projects-power-in-strategic-south-china-sea.html?pagewanted=all.

Kaufman, Stephen. "Clinton Urges Resolution of South China Sea Dispute." America.gov, July 23, 2010. http://www.america.gov/st/peacesec-english/2010/July/201 00723154256esnamfuak4.879177e-03.html.

Kai, He. "Does ASEAN Matter? International Relations Theories, Institutional Realism, and ASEAN." *Asian Security* 2, no. 3 (2006): 189–214.

Keith, Ronald C. "China as a Rising World Power and Its Response to 'Globalization'." *Review of International Affairs* 3, no. 4 (2004).

Khanna, Parag, and John Gilman. "Does Norway hold key to solving South China Sea dispute?" CNN, November 13, 2012. http://www.cnn.com/2012/11/13/opinion/khanna-south-china-sea-dispute/index.html.

Kissenger, Henry. *On China*. New York: Penguin Press HC, 2011.

Kivimaki, Timo. *War or Peace in the South China Sea?* Copenhagen: Nordic Institute of Asian Studies, 2002.

Klare, Michael. *Resource Wars: The New Landscape of Global Conflict*. New York: Henry Holt and Company, LLC, 2001.

Knut, Snildal. "Petroleum in the South China Sea—a Chinese National Interest?" Thesis, Department of Political Science, University of Oslo, June 2000.

Kondapalli, Srikanth. "The Chinese Military Eyes South Asia." In *Shaping China's Security Environment: The Role of The People's Liberation Army*, edited by Andrew Scobell and Larry Wortzel, 198–282. Carlisle, PA: Strategic Studies Institute, U.S. Army War College, 2006.

Krishna, S. M. "Ties with China Priority of India's Foreign Policy." *Daily News and Analysis*, June 6, 2012. http://www.dnaindia.com/india/report_ties-with-china-priority-of-india-s-foreign-policy-sm-krishna_1699011.

Krishnan, Ananth. "China Warns India in South China Sea Exploration Projects." *The Hindu*, September 15, 2011. http://www.thehindu.com/news/international/article2455647.ece.

Kurlantzick, Joshua. *Charm Offensive: How China's Soft Power Is Transforming the World*. New Haven, Connecticut: Yale University Press, 2007.

Landler, Mark. "Offering to Aid Talks, U.S. Challenges China on Disputed Islands." *The New York Times*, July 23, 2010. http://www.nytimes.com/2010/07/24/world/asia/24diplo.html.

Lee-Brago, Pia. "China Insists on Bilateral Talks on Spratlys." *Philippine Star*, April 11, 2012. http://www.philstar.com/headlines/795514/china-insists-bilateral-talks-spratlys-row.

Leifer, Michael. *ASEAN and the Security of Southeast Asia*. London: Routledge, 1989.

———. "Truth about the Balance of Power, in the Evolving Pacific Power Structure." In *Evolving Pacific Power Structures*, edited by Derek de Cunha, 47–51. Singapore: Institute of Southeast Asian Studies, 1996.

———. *Selected Works on Southeast Asia*. Singapore: Institute of Southeast Asian Studies, 2005.

Livezey, William E. *Mahan on Sea Power*. Norman, OK: University of Oklahoma Press, 1981.

Livingstone, David. "The Spratly Islands: A Regional Perspective." *Journal of the Washington Institute of China Studies* 1, no. 2 (Fall 2006): 149–60.

Liyao, Ma. "Indian Report Points to China's growing military capabilities." *China Daily*, March 24, 2011. http://www.chinadaily.com.cn/cndy/2011-03/24/content_12218839.htm.

Los Angeles Times. "China Creates City on Disputed Island, Angering Neighbors." July 24, 2012.

Loy, Irwin. "South China Sea High on ASEAN Agenda." *Voice of America*, July 9, 2012. http://www.voanews.com/content/cambodia_says_asean_ministers_agree_key_elements_of_sea_code/1381394.html.

Macartney, Jane. "Chinese and American ships clash again in Yellow Sea." *Sunday Times*, May 6, 2009. http://www.infowars.com/chinese-and-american-ships-clash-again/.

Manicom, James. "Beyond Boundary Disputes: Understanding The Nature of China's Challenge to Maritime East Asia." *Harvard Asia Quarterly* 12, no. 3/4 (2011): 46–53.

———. "IR Theory and Asia's Maritime Territorial Disputes." Paper presented to the Australasian Political Studies Association Conference, University of Newcastle, September 2006.

Marlay, Ross. 1997. "China, the Philippines, and the Spratly Islands." *Asian Affairs: An American Review* 23, no. 4 (1997): 195–210.

Marvin, Taylor. "PRC Area-Denial Capabilities and American Power Projection." Prospect's Blog, June 8, 2012. http://smokeandstir.org/2012/06/08/prc-area-denial-capabilities-and-american-power-projection-part-1/.

McDonald, Mark. "East Asia's Sea Disputes: Scar Tissue from War Wounds." IHT Rendezvous, August 16, 2012. http://rendezvous.blogs.nytimes.com/2012/08/16/east-asias-sea-disputes-scar-tissue-from-war-wounds/.

Milivojevic, Marko. "The Spratly and Paracel Islands Conflict." *Survival* 31, no. 1 (January–February 1989): 70–8.

Military.com. "China's String of Pearls (East and South Asia)." Last modified June 21, 2011. http://forums.military.com/eve/forums/a/tpc/f/8001934822/m/1970017472001.

Mingjiang, Dr. Li. "Functional Cooperation and Pan-Beibu Gulf: Potential for Peace in the South China Sea." In *The South China Sea: Cooperation For Regional Security and Development: Proceedings of the International Workshop co-organized by the Diplomatic Academy of Vietnam and the Vietnam Lawyers' Association*, edited by Tran Truong Thuy, 290–304. Hanoi: Diplomatic Academy of Vietnam, November 2009. http://nghiencuubiendong.vn/en/datbase-on-south-china-sea-study/doc_details/36-the-south-china-sea-cooperation-for-regional-security-and-development.

Ministry of Foreign Affairs of the People's Republic of China. "China's Indisputable Sovereignty Over the Xisha and Nansha Islands." *Beijing Review* 7 (January 30, 1980).

Ministry of Foreign Affairs, Socialist Republic of Vietnam. "The Hoang Sa and Truong Sa Archipelagos and International Law." Hanoi, April 1988.

Modelski, George and William R. Thompson. *Seapower in Global Politics, 1494–1993*. Seattle, WA: University of Washington Press, 1988.

Moller, Kay. "Cambodia and Burma: The ASEAN Way Ends Here." *Asian Survey* 38, no. 12 (1998): 1087–1104.

Morse, Eric S. "Geopolitics in the South China Sea and Indian Ocean Region: Tiny Ripples or Shifting Tides?" National Strategy Forum Review Blog, August 30, 2010. www.nationalstrategy.com.

National Bureau of Asian Research. Pacific Energy Summit: Unlocking the Potential of Natural Gas in the Asia-Pacific, 2011 Summit Report. Seattle, WA: National Bureau of Asian Research, 2011. http://www.nbr.org/downloads/pdfs/ETA/PES2011_summitreport.pdf.

Nesadurai, Helen. *Globalization and Economic Security in East Asia*. London: Routledge, 2005.

New York Times. "Economic Juggernaut: China is Passing US as Asian Power." *New York Times*, June 29, 2002.

———. "Under Diplomatic Strain, Japan Recalls Envoy in Dispute With China Over Islands." *New York Times*, July 15, 2012.

Nguyen, Dong Manh. "Settlement of Disputes under the 1982 United Nations Convention on the Law of the Sea: The Case of the South China Sea Dispute." UN-Nippon Foundation, New York, December 2005.

Nguyen, Thao and Amer Ramses. "A New Legal Arrangement for the South China Sea?" *Ocean Development & International Law* 40 (2009): 333–49.

Ning, Lu. *The Spratly Archipelago: The Origins of the Claims and Possible Solutions*. Washington, DC: International Center, 1993.

Nischalk, Tobias. "Does ASEAN Measure Up? Post-Cold War Diplomacy and the Idea of Regional Community." *The Pacific Review* 12, no. 1 (2002): 89–117.

Num, Mak Joon. "Sovereignty in ASEAN and the Problem of Maritime Cooperation in the South China Sea." In *Security and International Politics in the South China Sea: Towards a Co-operative Management Regime*, edited by Sam Bateman and Ralf Emmers. London: Routledge, 2009.

———. "Sovereignty in ASEAN and the Problem of Maritime Cooperation in the South China Sea." Working Paper No. 156, S. Rajaratnam School of International Studies, Singapore, 2008. http://www.isn.ethz.ch/isn/Digital-Library/Publications/Detail/?ots591=cab359a3-9328-19cc-a1d2-8023e646b22c&lng=en&id=55374.

Odgaard, Liselotte. "Conflict Control and Crisis Management between China and Southeast Asia: an Analysis of the Workshops on Managing Potential Conflicts in the South China Sea." Draft Paper, Department of Political Science, Aarhus University, 1999. http://citeseerx.ist.psu.edu/viewdoc/summary?doi=10.1.1.37.657.

———. "Deterrence and Cooperation in the South China Sea." *Contemporary Southeast Asia* 23, no. 2 (August 2001): 292–306.

Office of the Secretary of Defense. Military and Security Developments Involving the People's Republic of China 2010: A Report to Congress Pursuant to the National Defense Authorization Act for Fiscal Year 2010. United States Department of Defense. 2011, http://www.defense.gov/pubs/pdfs/2011_CMPR_Final.pdf.

Ojendal, Joakim. "Southeast Asia at a Constant Crossroads Southeast Asia at a Constant Crossroads: An Ambiguous 'New Region.'" In *Regionalization in a Globalizing World: A Comparative Perspective on Forms, Actors and Processes*, edited by Michael Schulz, Fredrik Söderbaum, and Joakim Öjendal. London: Zed, 2001.

Opinion Asia. "The South China Sea Dispute: An Unbalanced Bargaining Game by Du Tran," February 9, 2009.

Pant, Harsh V. "South China Sea: New Arena of Sino-Indian Rivalry: China Ignores India's Exploration, Puts Vietnam's Oil Block Up for Global Bid." YaleGlobal, August 2, 2012. http://yaleglobal.yale.edu/content/south-china-sea-new-arena-sino-indian-rivalry.

Pao, Chang. "A New Scramble for the South China Sea Islands." *Contemporary Southeast Asia* 12, no. 1 (June 1990): 20–39.

Parameswaran, Prasanth. "Why the US-ASEAN Sunnylands Summit Matters?" *The Diplomat*, February 11, 2016. http://thediplomat.com/2016/02/why-the-us-asean-sunnylands-summit-matters/.

Pedrozo, Raul. "Close Encounters at Sea: The USNS Impeccable Incident." *Naval War College Review* 62, no. 3 (Summer 2009): 101–11.

Perlez, Jane. "Beijing Exhibiting New Assertiveness in South China Sea." *New York Times*, May 31, 2012. http://www.nytimes.com/2012/06/01/world/asia/beijing-projects-power-in-strategic-south-china-sea.html?pagewanted=all&_r=0.

———."Singaporean Tells China U.S. Is Not in Decline." *New York Times*, September 6, 2012. http://www.nytimes.com/2012/09/07/world/asia/singapores-prime-minister-warns-china-on-view-of-us.html.

———. "Alarm as China Issues Rules for Disputed Area." *New York Times*, December 1, 2012. http://www.nytimes.com/2012/12/02/world/asia/alarm-as-china-issues-rules-for-disputed-sea.html?r=0.

Philling, David. "Asia's Quiet Anger with 'Big, Bad' China." *Financial Times*, June 2, 2011. http://www.ft.com/intl/cms/s/0/da3396b6-8c81-11e0-883f-00144feab49a.html.

Prescott, John. *The Maritime Political Boundaries of the World.* New York: Methuen, 1985.

———. "Straight and Archipelagic Baselines." In *Maritime Boundaries and Ocean Resources*, edited by Gerald Blake. Lanham, MD: Rowman & Littlefield Publishers, 1987.

Promfret, John. "Beijing claims 'indisputable sovereignty' over South China." *Washington Post*, July 31, 2010. http://www.washingtonpost.com/wp-dyn/content/article/2010/07/30/AR2010073005664.html.

Rakesh, Sharma. "Oil Firms in China And India Pull Closer." *Wall Street Journal*, June 19, 2012. http://online.wsj.com/article/SB100014240527023038364045774 76090216555460.html.

Ramli, Nik. "Troubled Waters in the South China Sea." *Biuletyn Opinie*, April 13, 2010. http://www.kwasniewskialeksander.eu/attachments/BIULETYN_OPINIE_FAE_Troubled_Waters_in_the_South_China_Sea.pdf.

Rand Corporation. "The United States and Asia: Toward a New U.S. Strategy and Force Posture." Project Air Force Report, 2001.

Raymond, Catherine Zara. "Piracy and Armed Robbery in the Malacca Strait: A Problem Solved?" *Naval War College Review* 62, no. 3 (2009).

Reubel, Robert C. "Is China the real Mahanian maritime power of the 21st century?" Information Dissemination: The Intersection of Maritime Strategy and Strategic Communications. June 12, 2012. http://www.informationdissemination.net/2012/06/is-china-real-mahanian-maritime-power.html.

Reuters. "China Tests Troubled Waters with $1 bln Rig for South China Sea." June 21, 2012. http://www.reuters.com/article/2012/06/21/us-china-southchinasea-idUSBRE85K03Y20120621.

———. "India Army Chief Wary of Growing China Military." July 4, 2004. http://dev-bd.bdnews24.com/details.php?id=107347&cid=1.

Richardson, Michael. "In Knots and Tangles Over Freedom of the Sea." *The Straits Times*, July 28, 2010. http://www.iseas.edu.sg/viewpoint/mr28jul10.pdf.

———. "Commentary on Energy and Geopolitics in the South China Sea by Michael Richardson." http://www.iseas.edu.sg/aseanstudiescentre/ascdf2c1.pdf.

Rodrigue, Jean-Paul. "Straits, Passages and Chokepoints: A Maritime Geostrategy of Petroleum Distribution." *Cahiers de Géographie du Québec* 48, no. 135 (December 2004): 357–74.

Rosenberg, David. "Review of ASEAN-China Relations: Realities and Prospects," edited by Saw Swee-Hock, Sheng Lijun and Chin Kin Wah. *The China Journal* 56 (July 2006): 229–31. http://community.middlebury.edu/~scs/docs/Rosenberg,%20David.ASEAN-China%20Relations-Review.pdf.

———. "Governing The South China Sea: From Freedom of The Seas to Ocean Enclosure Movements." *Harvard Asia Quarterly* (Winter 2010): 4–12.

Rosenberg, David and Christopher Chung. "Maritime Security in the South China Sea: Coordinating Coastal and User State Priorities." *Ocean Development and International Law* 39 (2008): 51–68.

Roy, Nalanda. "Indonesia Today: A Story of Bitter Dawn." Master's thesis, Jadavpur University, India, 2004.

Saighal, Maj. Gen. (rtd) Vinod. "International Workshop on 'South China Sea: Cooperation for Security and Development'." In *The South China Sea: Cooperation For Regional Security and Development: Proceedings of the International Workshop*

Co-organized by the Diplomatic Academy of Vietnam and the Vietnam Lawyers' Association, edited by Tran Truong Thuy, 7–14. Hanoi: Diplomatic Academy of Vietnam, November 2009. http://nghiencuubiendong.vn/en/datbase-on-south-china-sea-study/doc_details/36-the-south-china-sea-cooperation-for-regional-security-and-development.

Saleem, Omar. "The Spratly Islands Dispute: China Defines the New Millennium." *American University Law Review* 15, no. 3 (2000): 527–82.

Schippke, Wolfgang. "The History of the Spratly Islands in the South China Sea." http://www.southchinasea.org/docs/Schippke/1s0_h.html.

Schofield, Clive, ed. "Maritime energy resources in Asia, Legal Regimes and Cooperation." *NBR Special Report*, no. 37 (February 2012).

Segal, Gerald and Richard Yang, eds. *Chinese Economic Reform: The Impact on Security*. London: Routledge, 1996.

Sen, Sudhi Ranjan. "Indian Navy Will Intervene in South China Sea, If Required." NDTV (India) December 3, 2012. http://www.ndtv.com/article/india/indian-navy-will-intervene-in-south-china-sea-if-required-300388.

Serizawa, Sarah. "China's Military Modernization and Implications for Northeast Asia: An Interview with Christopher W. Hughes," National Bureau of Asian Research, August 2, 2012. http://www.nbr.org/research/activity.aspx?id=266.

Severino, Rodolfo. *Southeast Asia in Search of an ASEAN Community: Insights from the Former ASEAN Secretary-General*. Singapore: ISEAS, 2006.

Shee, Kim. "The South China Sea in China's Strategic Thinking." *Contemporary Southeast Asia* 19, no. 4 (March 1998): 369–87.

Sheldon, Simon. "US-Southeast Asia Relations: Deep in South China Sea Diplomacy, Comparative Connections." *A Triannual E-Journal on East Asian Bilateral Relations* (September 2011). http://www.isn.ethz.ch/isn/Digital-Library/Publications/Detail/?lng=en&id=134934.

Shepharp, Allen. "Maritime Tensions in the South China Sea and the Neighborhood: Some Solutions." *Studies in Conflict and Terrorism* 21, no. 2 (April–June 1994): 209–11.

Singh, Amit. "South China Sea Dispute and India." National Maritime Foundation, June 20, 2012.

Singh, Jaswant. "Asia's Giants Colliding at Sea?" Project Syndicate, October 24, 2011. http://www.project-syndicate.org/commentary/asia-s-giants-colliding-at-sea.

Smith, Esmond D. "China's Aspirations in the Spratly Islands." *Contemporary Southeast Asia* 16, no. 3 (December 1994): 274–94.

Smith, Robert W. "Joint (Development) Zones: A Review of Past Practice and Thoughts on the Future." In *Sustainable Development and Preservation of the Oceans: The Challenges of UNCLOS and Agenda 21*, edited by Mochtar Kusuma-Atmadja, Thomas A. Mensah and Bernard H. Oxman. Honolulu: The Law of the Sea Institute, University of Hawaii, 1997.

Snyder, Scott. "The SCS Dispute: Prospects for Preventive Diplomacy." Special Report No. 18 of the United States Institute of Peace (August 1996).

Song, Yann-Huei. "The Overall Situation in the South China Sea in the New Millennium: Before and After the September 11 Terrorist Attacks." *Ocean Development and International Law* 34 (2003): 229–77.

Stanslas, Pooja. "The Spratly Dilemma: External powers and Dispute Resolution Mechanisms." *Biuletyn Opinie* 34 (November 2, 2010).

Stenseth, Leni. "Nationalism and Foreign Policy—The Case of China's Nansha Rhetoric." Phd Dissertation, University of Oslo, 1998.

Stevenson, Jim. "Turbulence Remains in South China Sea." Voice of America.com, October 17, 2010.

Storey, Ian James. "Creeping Assertiveness: China, the Philippines and the South China Sea Dispute." *Contemporary Southeast Asia* 21, no. 1 (1999): 95–118.

———. "Conflict in the South China Sea: China's Relations with Vietnam and the Philippines." *China Brief* 8, no. 8 (April 14, 2008).

———. "China's 'Malacca Dilemma'." *The Jamestown Foundation China Brief* 6, no. 8 (April 12, 2006).

Swaine, Michael D., and Ashley J. Tellis. *Interpreting China's Grand Strategy Past, Present, and Future.* Santa Monica, CA: RAND Corporation, 2000. http://www.rand.org/pubs/monograph_reports/MR1121.html.

Swanstrom, Niklas. "Conflict Management and Negotiations in the South China Sea: The ASEAN Way?" Online publication of the Virtual Library of South China Sea, 1999. http://community.middlebury.edu/~scs/docs/Swanstrom.pdf.

Swanstrom, Niklas, ed. *Asia 2018–2028: Development Scenarios.* Nacka, Sweden: Institute for Security and Development Policy, June 2008.

Swee-Hock, Saw, Sheng Lijun, and Chin KinWah, eds. *ASEAN-China Relations: Realities and Prospects.* Singapore: Institute of Southeast Asian Studies, 2005.

Taipei Times. "PRC starts combat-ready patrols in South China Sea." *Taipei Times*, June 29, 2012. http://www.taipeitimes.com/News/front/archives/2012/06/29/2003536519.

Tan, Tony. "Policing the Sea Is a Job for Everyone." *Straits Times*, June 3, 2003.

Taylor, Marvin. "PRC Area-Denial Capabilities and American Power Projection." Prospect's Blog (June 2012). http://prospectjournalblog.wordpress.com/.

Tellis, Ashley J., Travis Tanner and Jessica Keough, eds. *Strategic Asia 2011–12: Asia Responds to Its Rising Powers—China and India.* Seattle, WA: National Bureau of Asian Research, 2011.

Thayer, Carlyle A. "Recent Developments in the South China Sea: Implications for Peace, Stability and Cooperation in the Region." In *The South China Sea: Cooperation For Regional Security and Development: Proceedings of the International Workshop co-organized by the Diplomatic Academy of Vietnam and the Vietnam Lawyers' Association*, edited by Tran Truong Thuy, 125–138. Hanoi: Diplomatic Academy of Vietnam, November 2009. http://nghiencuubiendong.vn/en/datbase-on-south-china-sea-study/doc_details/36-the-south-china-sea-cooperation-for-regional-security-and-development.

———. "The United States and Chinese Assertiveness in the South China Sea." *Security Challenges* 6, no. 2 (Winter 2010): 69–84.

———. "China's New Wave of Aggressive Assertiveness in the South China Sea." Online Paper, Center for Strategic and International Studies, Washington, DC, June 30, 2011. http://csis.org/publication/chinas-new-wave-aggressive-assertiveness-south-china-sea.

———. "Sovereignty Disputes in the South China Sea: Diplomacy, Legal Regimes, and Realpolitik." Paper presented at the International Conference on Topical Regional Security Initiatives in East Asia, St. Petersburg University, St. Petersburg, Russian Federation, April 6–7, 2012.

———. "Diplomatic Currents Running Strong in the South China Sea." *East Asia Forum*, April 4, 2012. http://www.eastasiaforum.org/2012/04/04/diplomatic-currents-running-strong-in-the-south-china-sea/.

———. "Is the Philippines an orphan?" *The Diplomat*, May 2, 2012. http://thediplomat.com/2012/05/02/is-the-philippines-an-orphan/.

———. "Standoff in the South China Sea Scarborough Shoal Standoff Reveals Blunt Edge of China's Peaceful Rise." *Yale Global*, June 12, 2012. http://yaleglobal.yale.edu/content/standoff-south-china-sea.

Thomas, Jim. "China's Active Defense Strategy and Its Regional Implications." Testimony Before The U.S.–China Economic And Security Review Commission. January 2011. http://www.csbaonline.org/publications/2011/01/chinas-active-defense-strategy-and-its-implications/2/.

Thuy, Tran Truong. "Recent Developments in the South China Sea: Implications for Regional Security and Cooperation." Washington, DC: Center for Strategic and International Studies/CSIS, 2006. http://csis.org/publication/recent-developments-south-china-sea-implications-regional-security-and-cooperation.

Till, Geoffrey. "The South China Sea Dispute: An International History." In *Security and International Politics in the South China Sea: Towards a Co-operative Management Regime*, edited by Sam Bateman and Ralf Emmers. London: Routledge, 2009.

———. "South China Sea: Just Waiting for the Breeze." In *The South China Sea: Cooperation For Regional Security and Development: Proceedings of the International Workshop co-organized by the Diplomatic Academy of Vietnam and the Vietnam Lawyers' Association*, edited by Tran Truong Thuy, 15–21. Hanoi: Diplomatic Academy of Vietnam, November 2009. http://nghiencuubiendong.vn/en/datbase-on-south-china-sea-study/doc_details/36-the-south-china-sea-cooperation-for-regional-security-and-development.

Times of India. "China Warns US from 'Muddying Waters' in South China Sea." June 3, 2012. http://articles.timesofindia.indiatimes.com/2012-06-03/china/32005634_1_south-china-sea-naval-fleet-china-claims.

———. "China to Deploy Drones to Conduct Maritime Surveillance." August 29, 2012. http://articles.timesofindia.indiatimes.com/2012-08-29/china/33475416_1_maritime-disputes-drones-state-oceanic-administration.

Tonnesson, Stein. "China and the South China Sea: A Peace Proposal." *Security Dialogue* 31, no. 3 (2000): 307–26.

———. "The History of the Dispute." In *War or Peace in the South China Sea?* edited by Timo Kivimaki. Copenhagen: NIAS Press, 2002.

———. "China's Boomerang Diplomacy: China's Treatment of East Asian Neighbors Hits Back and Undermines its Peaceful Development." *Yale Global*, November 16, 2012. http://yaleglobal.yale.edu/content/chinas-boomerang-diplomacy.

Townsend-Gault, Ian. "Maritime Cooperation in a Functional Perspective," *National Bureau of Asian Research*, Special Report no. 37 (February 2012).

Townshend, Ashley S. "Unraveling China's 'String of Pearls'." *Yale Global*, September 16, 2011. http://yaleglobal.yale.edu/content/unraveling-chinas-string-of-pearls.

U.S. Energy Information Administration. "Country Analysis Briefs: South China Sea Region." September 2003. http://apps.americanbar.org/intlaw/committees/industries/energy_natural_resources/schina.pdf.

————. "China: Country Analysis Brief." September 4, 2012. http://www.eia.gov/countries/analysisbriefs/China/china.pdf.

————. "World Oil Transit Chokepoints." Last modified August 22, 2012. http://www.eia.gov/countries/analysisbriefs/World_Oil_Transit_Chokepoints/wotc.pdf.

————. "South China Sea." Last modified February 7, 2013. http://www.eia.gov/countries/analysisbriefs/South_China_Sea/south_china_sea.pdf.

U.S. Marine Corps. "A Cooperative Strategy for 21st Century Seapower." October 2007. http://www.navy.mil/maritime/Maritimestrategy.pdf.

Vannarith, Cheang. "Asia Pacific Security Issues: Challenges and Adaptive Mechanism." *Cambodian Institute for Cooperation and Peace Policy Brief* 3 (July 2010).

Valencia, Mark. "The Spratly Islands: Dangerous Ground in the South China Sea." *The Pacific Review* 1, no. 4 (1988): 438–43.

————."The South China Sea: Back to the Future?" *Global Asia: A Journal of the East Asia Foundation* 5, no. 4 (December, 2010). http://www.globalasia.org/V5N4_Winter_2010/Mark_J_Valencia.html.

————. "Tempting the Dragon." *Policy Forum Online*, March 12, 2009. http://nautilus.org/napsnet/napsnet-policy-forum/tempting-the-dragon/#sect1.

————. "Regional Maritime Regime Building: Prospects in Northeast and Southeast Asia." *Ocean Development and International Law* 31 (2000): 223–47.

————. "Mischief at the Reef." *Far Eastern Economic Review* 162, no. 20 (May 20, 1999): 31.

————. "Whither the South China Sea Disputes?" Report Series No. 8: Energy and Geopolitics in the South China Sea: Implications for ASEAN and Its Dialogue Partners (Singapore: Asian Studies Centre Institute of Southeast Asian Studies, 2009). http://asc.iseas.edu.sg/images/stories/pdf/ASC8.pdf.

————. "The South China Sea Brouhaha: Separating Substance from Atmospherics." Policy Forum 10-044, Nautilus Institute for Security and Sustainability, August 10, 2010. http://nautilus.org/napsnet/napsnet-policy-forum/the-south-china-sea-brouhaha-separating-substance-from-atmospherics/.

Valencia, Mark, Jon M. Van Dyke, and Noel A. Ludwig. *Sharing the Resources of the South China Sea*. Leiden, The Netherlands: Martinus Nijhoff Publishers, 1997.

Van Auken, Bill. "Pentagon Chief Asserts US National Interest in China Seas." wsws.org. October 13, 2010. http://www.wsws.org/en/articles/2010/10/gate-o13.html.

Van Dyke, Jon M., and Dal Bennett. "Islands and the Delimitation of Ocean Space in the South China Sea." *Ocean Yearbook* 10 (1993): 55–6.

Vannarith, Chheang. "Asia Pacific Security Issues: Challenges and Adaptive Mechanism." *Cambodian Institute for Cooperation and Peace Policy Brief* 3 (July 2010). http://www.cicp.org.kh/download/CICP%20Policy%20brief/CICP%20Policy%20brief%20No%203.pdf.

Volkhonsky, Boris. "U.S. policy in the South China Sea." *Voice of Russia*. June 9, 2012. http://english.ruvr.ru/2012_06_09/77629409/.

Waldmeir, Patti and Kathrin Hille. "US and China argue over South China Sea." ft.com, August 5, 2012. http://www.ft.com/intl/cms/s/0/0c095378-dec6-11e1-b615-00144feab49a.html.

Washington Post. "China's Navy Engaging in Unprecedented Coordination with India, Japan on Anti-piracy Patrols." July 3, 2012.

Weatherbee, Donald. "The South China Sea: From Zone of Conflict to Zone of Peace?" In *East Asian Conflict Zones: Prospects for Regional Stability and De-escalation*, edited by Lawrence Grinter and Kihl Young. London: Macmillan Press, 1987.

Wei, Da. "Has China Become 'Tough'?" *China Security* 6, no. 3 (2010): 35–42.

Weiss, Stanley. "Rowing Between Two Reefs." *The New York Times*, August 30, 2010. http://www.nytimes.com/2010/08/31/opinion/31iht-edweiss.html?gwh=931A8D84C6764E888EE1735B33F8ED7D.

Wesley, Michael. "Meditating the Global Order: The Past and Future of Asia-Pacific Regional Organizations." In *Asia Pacific Security: Policy Challenges*, edited by David Lovell. Singapore: ISEAS, 2003.

White, Hugh. "Power Shift: Australia's Future between Washington and Berlin." *Quarterly Essay* 39 (September 2010). http://www.quarterlyessay.com/issue/power-shift-australia%E2%80%99s-future-between-washington-and-beijing.

Williams, Carol J. "China-U.S. Power Play at Core of East Asian Island Disputes." *Los Angeles Times*, September 12, 2012. http://latimesblogs.latimes.com/world_now/2012/09/china-us-power-play-at-core-of-east-asian-island-disputes.html.

Wong, Edward. "Freed From Shoals, Warship Heads Back to China." *New York Times*, July 16, 2012. http://www.nytimes.com/2012/07/17/world/asia/freed-from-shoals-warship-heads-back-to-china.html.

Wong, John. "New Dimensions in China-ASEAN Relations." In *China-ASEAN Relations: Economic and Legal Dimensions*, edited by John Wong. Hackensack, NJ: World Scientific Publishing Company, 2006.

Xiaofeng, Ren and Cheng Xizhong. "A Chinese Perspective." *Marine Policy* 29 (2005): 139–46.

Xinhua, english.news.cn. "Xinhua Insight: China manned sub may dive in South China Sea 2013." July 16, 2012. http://news.xinhuanet.com/english/indepth/2012-07/16/c_131718966.htm.

———. "Renaming of Area in South China Sea will not Affect China's Sovereignty." September 13, 2012. http://news.xinhuanet.com/english/china/2012-09/13/c_131848692.htm.

———. "China Publishes New Maps: South China Sea Islands Highlighted." January 11, 2013. http://news.xinhuanet.com/english/china/2013-01/11/c_132097207.htm.

Xu, Rui Song. "Petroleum and Gas Research by Remote Sensing In South China Sea." *Symposium on Geospatial Theory, Processing and Applications* 34, no. 4 (2002): 1–5.

Yee, Andy. "China and its territorial disputes: One approach does not fit all." *East Asia Forum*, January 20, 2011. http://www.eastasiaforum.org/2011/01/20/china-and-its-territorial-disputes-one-approach-does-not-fit-all/.

Yuan, Jing-Dong. *Asia-Pacific Security: China's Conditional Multilateralism and Great Power Entente*. Strategic Studies Institute, US Army War College, 2000.

Zha, Daojiong and Mark J. Valencia. "Mischief Reef: Geopolitics and Implications." *Journal of Contemporary Asia* 31, no. 1 (2001): 86–103.

Zou, Keyuan. "Historic Rights in International Law and in China's Practice." *Ocean Development and International Law* 32, no. 2 (2001): 149–68.

———. "Joint Development in the South China Sea: A New Approach." *The International Journal of Marine and Coastal Law* 21, no. 1 (2006): 83–109.

———. "Can China Respect The Law Of The Seas?: An Assessment Of Maritime Agreements Between China And Its Neighbors." *Harvard Asia Quarterly* (Winter 2010): 39–45.

Zubaidah Rahim, Lily. "Fragmented Community and Unconstructive Engagements: ASEAN and Burma's SPDC Regime." *Critical Asian Studies* 40, no. 1 (2008): 67–88.

Index

Index

About the Author

Nalanda Roy is an assistant professor at Armstrong State University (ASU) in Savannah, Georgia. Nalanda did her PhD from Rutgers-The State University of New Jersey in Global Affairs and masters in Sociology and Anthropology from the University of Toledo, Ohio. Nalanda also has a masters and MPhil in international relations from Jadavpur University, India. Her expertise lies in the field of international relations, comparative politics, globalization, and Asian politics. Nalanda is the associate editor for JASIA, SAGE, and serves on other editorial boards as well. Currently, Nalanda has been appointed by the City Council of Savannah as one of the board of directors for the Greater Savannah International Alliance (GSIA). Dr. Roy has published a book titled *Bitter Moments—The Story of Indonesian Fragmentation*, Minerva Associates (Publications), in 2015. She has presented her scholarly work at various national and international conferences, and her research has been widely recognized.